Black blood is sure powerful—because just one drop of Black blood makes you a Black man. One drop, you are Black. Black is powerful.
—Langston Hughes

Biography is the only history; History is the garb of biography.
—Thomas Carlyle

700 NOTABLE PERSONS OF
AFRICAN ANCESTRY
1400 BC TO PRESENT DAY

*An Eye-Opener of 3,400 Years of World
Black History*

Compiled by
Simon Burris

authorHOUSE®

AuthorHouse™
1663 Liberty Drive
Bloomington, IN 47403
www.authorhouse.com
Phone: 1 (800) 839-8640

Published by AuthorHouse 02/19/2018

ISBN: 978-1-5462-1212-6 (sc)
ISBN: 978-1-5462-1210-2 (hc)
ISBN: 978-1-5462-1211-9 (e)

Library of Congress Control Number: 2017915409

Contents

Introduction

This manuscript, published in a perpetual calendar form, is designed to acquaint you with well-documented historical facts concerning individuals of black and African ancestry. Some are famous and some are lesser known, but all are equally emphasizing their contributions to our modern civilization. This calendar narrative is solely about unearthing and revealing the black bloodline that extends far beyond skin pigmentation, nationality, or race.

What is unique about this publication is that we have included several prominent Europeans and European-Americans of the past and present who had or have black ancestors, however they are not commonly known as blacks or Africans.[1] There are thousands of persons who, by their achievements, merit mention here, but that would require volumes. Our objective is to profile a selection of some seven hundred entries for this calendar, providing a cross-section of personalities, professions, very brief synopses, bona fide birth data,[2] major events in chronological order, and some famous firsts. In addition, there are others whose deeds made history as well as news headlines enveloping each of the 366 days of the year. We've drawn from the annals of the United States, the Americas, Africa, Asia, Europe, and other areas of the world, with subjects of varying degrees of rank and prominence.

---

[1] All blacks are not Africans.
[2] Where birth date (b.) was not available, or was obscure or ambiguous, we have used date of death (d.), as well as Feast Day for canonized Christian saints.

True history has no color. Due to centuries of slavery, prejudices, and ingrained ignorance, "black history" as we know it ranks second to the Bible narrative, and it is the premier source of heralding and maintaining our rich and bountiful heritage. Please note that there are no slavery-era classifications utilized in this format regarding white or black admixture: half black (mulatto), one-fourth black (quadroon), one-eighth black (octoroon); negro, negroid, colored, person of color, pure-bred, mixed-blood (biracial). No attempt has been made to denote one's degree of black ethnicity, whether 99.9 percent or 0.1 percent. Neither are there archaic appellations such as Abyssinian, Berber, Creole, Maroon, Moor, Nubian, or Saracen. The terms *black, African* and *Hamite* are employed interchangeably and exclusively.

We hope this informational historical birthday calendar will serve as a Fortune 700 guidepost that will enlighten the general public of the inestimable accomplishments for the betterment of mankind gifted by individuals acknowledged in this work from yesteryear to the present day.

January

Historical facts are all pervasive and cut through the most rigid barrier of race and caste.

—John Hope Franklin

1

John Clarke (b. Union Springs, Alabama, 1915), scholar and pioneer in the creation of Africana Studies in the 1960s.

2

Oscar Micheaux (b. 1898)**,** first African American filmmaker. Micheaux wrote and produced fifty films from 1919 to 1948.

John Hope Franklin (b. 1915), historian and 1995 Presidential Medal of Freedom honoree.

3

William Tucker (b. 1621), first African child to be born in the English colony of America, Jamestown, Virginia.

Frederick K. C. Price (b. 1932), famed clergyman and author of *Race, Religion and Racism* (1999).

Marc Morial (b. 1958), former New Orleans mayor and president of National Urban League (2003).

4

Grace Bumby (b. St. Louis, Missouri, 1937), opera songstress whose career spanned some thirty years.

5

Alvin Ailey (b. Rogers, Texas, 1931), globally acclaimed choreographer and founder of the Alvin Ailey American Dance Theater in New York (1958).

6

John Singleton (b. Los Angeles, California, 1968), Oscar-nominated film director.

7

Frederick Gregory (b. Washington, DC, 1941), first African American astronaut. Gregory commanded the space shuttle *Challenger* mission (1978).
Lewis Hamilton (b. 1985), English-born racecar champion.

8

Nancy Jones (b. 1860), considered the first black American missionary in Angola (Africa) from 1888 to 1897.

9

Earl Graves (b. 1935), publisher and CEO *Black Enterprise* magazine (1970).

10

Miltiades (d. 314) saint and the thirty-second Roman pope, fourth of African descent. Roman persecution of Christians was terminated during his pontificate (311–314).[3]
George Washington Carver (b. Missouri, 1864), former slave, scientist, and inventor of some three hundred products, mainly developed from peanuts (such as peanut butter) and sweet potatoes.

---

[3] Feast Day: The Catholic Church assigns one date of the year to commemorate all canonized saints, typically the actual day of death.

11

Ar-Rahman III (b. 889), eighth king of Cordoba (Muslim Spain) from 912 to 929.

12

Mordecai Johnson (b. 1898), educator; the first black president of Howard University in 1926.

13

Charlotte Ray (b. 1850), New York City native who became America's first black female lawyer in 1872.

14

Julian Bond (b. 1940), influential NAACP chairman and Georgia state senator.

15

Martin Luther King Jr. (b. Atlanta, Georgia, 1929), great human rights leader who led 3,200 protestors on a 54-mile march from Selma to Montgomery for voting rights in 1965.

16

Fulgencio Batista (b. 1901), Cuban president; ousted by Fidel Castro in 1959.

17

Paul Cuffe (b. 1759), wealthy shipbuilder and leader of the "resettlement to Africa" movement, 1800s.

L. Douglas Wilder (b. 1931), first African American governor of Virginia, 1990 to 1994.

Muhammad Ali (b. Louisville, Kentucky, 1942), world-famous boxing champion and Muslim activist.

Michelle Obama (b. DeYoung, Illinois, 1964), America's *second* lady and wife of President Barack Obama.

18

Daniel Williams (b. Hollidaysburg, Pennsylvania, 1856), surgeon who performed first successful open-heart surgery in 1893.

19

John H. Johnson (b. 1918), distinguished publisher of *Ebony* and *Jet* magazines.

20

Eva Jessye (b. 1895), choral director; original chorus trainer for Gershwin's opera *Porgy and Bess* (1935).

21

Eric Holder (b. New York City, 1951), first African American US attorney general (2008–2015). Holder's parents were from Barbados.

22

Thomas Jennings (b. New York City, 1771), first black granted a patent for the original dry-cleaning device (1821).

23

Benjamin Chavis Jr. (b. Oxford, North Carolina, 1948), human rights activist and author.

24

John Burr (b. 1849), Maryland engineer and inventor of the rotary-blade lawnmower (1899).

25

Thomas J. Martin (b. 1843), inventor of the fire extinguisher (1872).

26

Bessie Coleman (b. Atlanta, Texas, 1892), first female pilot of African descent (1922).

27

Wilhelm II (b. 1859), last emperor of Germany (1888–1918); descendant of Charlotte Sophia and grandson of Queen Victoria.

28

Richard Barthe (b. 1901), notable Mississippian sculptor and painter.

29

Oprah Winfrey (b. Kosciusko, Mississippi, 1954), TV host, actress, humanitarian, and second black American billionaire.

30

Didius Julianus (b. AD 133), twentieth emperor of the Roman Empire (AD 193) and second of African descent; had African mother.

Sojourner Truth (b. 1797), Slavery escapee at age twenty-nine. As an abolitionist, she raised funds for the Union Army.

31

Jackie Robinson (b. Cairo, Georgia, 1919), broke Major League Baseball's race barrier (1947).

Noel Jones (b. Jamaica, 1950), Pentecostal bishop (1994) and charismatic pastor of the City of Refuge Church in Gardena, California.

George Washington Carver

Sojourner Truth

Jackie Robinson

First Lady Michelle Obama

February

I've missed more than nine thousand shots in my career. I've lost almost three hundred games. Twenty-six times I've been trusted to take the game winning shot and missed. I've failed over and over again in my life. And that is why I succeed.

—Michael Jordan

1

Francis Cardoza (b. 1836), secretary of state of South Carolina (1868) and the first black official of any US state.

Langston Hughes (b. Joplin, Missouri, 1903), poet and fiction writer.

2

Pete Brown (b. 1935), golfer and first African American PGA Tour winner (1964).

3

Joao Café (b. 1935), president of Brazil (1954–1956).

4

Rosa Parks (b. Tuskegee, Alabama, 1913), crusader called the modern "first lady of civil rights."

5

Henry "Hank" Aaron (b. Mobile, Alabama, 1934), Major League Baseball hall of famer and home run king (1974).

6

Bonnie Coleman (b. 1945), US congresswoman from New Jersey (2015).

7

Abraham Van Salee (b. 1607), first permanent settler and wealthy landholder of Manhattan, New York City. Nicknamed "the Mulatto," he was the son of the Dutchman Jan Janszoon and his African secondary wife, Margarita.[4]

8

Elizabeth Wright (b. 1896), physician and homeopath.

9

Alice Walker (b. 1944), Pulitzer Prize–winning novelist for *The Color Purple* (1983).

10

Leontyne Price (b. Laurel, Mississippi, 1927), internationally acclaimed opera soprano.

11

Daniel "Chappie" James Jr. (b. 1920), first black four-star general of the US Army (1975).
Manuel Noriega (b. 1934), president of Panama (1983–1989).

12

Todd Duncan (b. 1944), premier singer who starred in the opera *Porgy and Bess*.

---

[4] Secondary wife: a concubine or mistress.

13

Absalom Jones (b. Sussex, Delaware, 1746), first black minister and priest ordained in America (1804).

Mal Goode (b. 1908), first African American television news correspondent (1962).

14

Richard Allen (b. Philadelphia, Pennsylvania, 1760), cofounder (with Absalom Jones) of the AME Church (1794); first black American bishop (1816).

Frederick Douglass (b. Talbot County, Maryland, 1817), former slave, abolitionist, and founder of Tuskegee Institute (1881).

Clarence Radford (b. Broken Bow, Oklahoma, 1934), renowned mathematician.

15

Mary Peake (b. 1823), educator, humanitarian, and cofounder of Hampton University (1868).

16

James Baskett (b. 1904), first black actor to receive an Academy Award (honorary, 1946).

17

Huey Newton (b. New Orleans, Louisiana, 1942), a founder of the Black Panther party in Oakland, California (1966).

Michael Jordan (b. Brooklyn, New York, 1963), basketball great and billionaire sportsman.

18

Paul R. Williams (b. 1894), architect and codesigner of Los Angeles Airport and Hollywood celebrities' homes.

Toni Morrison (b. Lorain, Ohio, 1931), novelist and author of *Beloved*.

Mayann Francis (b. 1946), lieutenant governor of Nova Scotia, Canada (2006–2012).

19

Clodius Albinus (d. 197), Roman usurper who ruled over Britain, Spain, and Portugal (AD 193–196).

20

Gloria Vanderbilt (b. New York City, 1924), heiress, designer of blue jeans, and a descendant of Abraham Van Salee.

Sidney Poitier (b. Miami, Florida, 1924), Bahamian American; first black to win Academy Award for Best Actor (1964).

21

John Lewis (b. 1940), Georgian congressman and civil rights activist.

22

Robert Franklin Jr. (b. 1954), president of Morehouse College (2004–2007).

23

W. E. B. DuBois (b. 1868), scholar, writer, and a cofounder of the NAACP.

Daymond John (b. Brooklyn, New York, 1969), entrepreneur, TV personality on *Shark Tank*.

24

Daniel Payne (b. 1811), reformer and co-founder of Wilberforce University in Ohio (1856).

Floyd Mayweather (b. Grand Rapids, Michigan, 1977), champion boxer in four different weight classes.

25

Sarah Boone (b. 1832), inventor of the ironing board (1892).

26

Elizabeth Keckley (b. 1818), seamstress of First Lady Mary Todd Lincoln.

Wallace Fard (b. 1877), founder of the Nation of Islam, 1930.

27

Patrick Healy (b. 1834), first black Jesuit priest and president of a white college, Georgetown University (1874–1882).

Marian Anderson (b. Philadelphia, Pennsylvania, 1897), concert singer and diplomat.

28

George Liele (b. 1752), emancipated slave and America's first Christian missionary, working in Jamaica (1782).

29

George Bridgetower (b. Poland, 1780), violinist who accompanied Beethoven.

Vinnie Johnson (b. Louisiana, 1920), musician and folklorist.

Frederick Douglas

Patrick Healy

March

You can cage the singer but not the song.

—Harry Belafonte

1

Blanche Bruce (b. Farmville, Virginia, 1841), Mississippi's second African American US Senator (1875–1881); was tutored by his white half-brother.

Harry Belafonte (b. New York City, 1927), world-famed performer.

2

Frank Peterson (b. Topeka, Kansas, 1932), US Marines Corps first black pilot (1952) and general (1979).

3

Alexander Crummell (b. 1819), Episcopal priest; moved to Liberia in 1853 and converted Africans to Christianity.

Charles Brooks (b. 1865), inventor of the mechanical street sweeper (1896).

4

Garrett Morgan (b. Paris, Kentucky, 1875), inventor of the gas mask (used in World War I) and the automatic traffic light.

5

Crispus Attucks (b. Massachusetts, 1723), first to die in the Boston Massacre (1770).

6

Elizabeth Barrett Browning (b. 1806), prominent English Victorian-era poetess.
English and West Indian parentage
Benjamin Arnett (b. 1839), influential advisor to President William McKinley.
James Edwards (b. Muncie, Indiana, 1918), first African American top-billing film actor (1940s).

7

Geta (b. 189), twenty-third Roman emperor (209–211); fifth of African descent. Younger son of Severus, from the Severan Dynasty.
Lynn Swann (b. 1952), Pittsburgh Steelers footballer and University of Southern California athletic director (2016).

8

Charles Kennybrew (b. Broken Bow, Oklahoma, 1932), Baptist minister, civic activist.
Lester Holt (b. Marin County, California, 1959), television host and journalist.

9

Roscoe Brown (b. 1922), Tuskegee Airmen commander during World War II.

10

Bayard Rustin (b. 1910), activist; initiated the first civil rights "Freedom Rides" (1947).

11

Thutmose III (d. 1425 BC), Egyptian pharaoh from 1479 to 1425 BC. Great empire builder at the time of Moses and the exodus.

Elagabalus (d. 222), twenty-fifth emperor of Rome (218–222), and seventh of African descent. Severan Dynasty

12

Charles Young (b. Mays Lick, Kentucky, 1864), third black West Point graduate (1889); army colonel in the Spanish American War.

Andrew Young (b. New Orleans, Louisiana, 1932), former mayor of Atlanta, Georgia; statesman and diplomat.

13

Idris (b. 1889), the first and only king of Libya (1950–1969).

Michael Curry (b. Chicago, Illinois, 1953), Episcopalian priest; elected presiding bishop of the Episcopal Church (2015).

14

Mildred Blount (b. 1907), innovative Hollywood milliner and designer; notable film credits include *Gone with the Wind* (1939) and *Easter Parade* (1948).

15. Joseph Roberts (b. Norfolk, Virginia, 1809), American-born first president of Liberia, elected in 1848.

16

Thomas Turner (b. 1877), cell biologist, Roman Catholic activist.

17

Norbert Rillieux (b. New Orleans, Louisiana, 1806), revolutionary inventor of the sugar refining evaporator (1846).

18

Charley Pride (b. Sledge, Mississippi, 1939), Country Hall of Fame singer.

Vanessa Williams (b. Tarrytown, New York, 1963), singer, actress, and beauty pageant queen; crowned Miss New York and Miss America in 1984.

19

Jackie "Moms" Mabley (b. 1887), veteran standup comedienne.

20

Willie Brown (b. Mineola, Texas, 1934), premier California legislator and San Francisco mayor.

21

Henry O. Flipper (b. Thomasville, Georgia, 1856), ex-slave and the first African American graduate from West Point (1856).

Anthony Overton (b. 1865), pioneer businessman and lawyer; established the Douglass National Bank in Chicago, Illinois (1923).

22

George Alcorn (b. 1940), nuclear physicist; invented the imaging X-ray spectrometer, 1984.

23

Maynard Jackson (b. 1938), first African American mayor of Atlanta, Georgia (1973).

24

Dorothy Height (b. Richmond, Virginia, 1912), women's rights advocate.

25

Thomas Alexandre Dumas (b. Haiti, 1762), Napoleonic general; had a Haitian mother and French father.

26

Tom Davis, Jr. (b. Houston, Texas, 1933), educator, author, and mentor.

27

Arthur Mitchell (b. 1934), choreographer; founder of Dance Theatre of Harlem (1969).

28

Harriet Tubman (b. 1819), Underground Railroad agent; led over three hundred enslaved people to freedom; first black American to appear on US paper money (2016).

29

James Chase (b. 1914), mayor of Spokane, Washington (1982–1986).

30

Moses Maimonides (b. Cordova, Spain, 1138), influential Hamitic (black) Jewish philosopher and physician in the Middle Ages.

31

Jack Johnson (b. Galveston, Texas, 1878), first African American world heavyweight boxing champion (1908 to 1915).

Harriet Tubman

Henry O. Flipper

April

Try to be a rainbow in someone's cloud.

—Maya Angelou

1

Clatonia Dorticus (b. 1856), Cuban-born inventor of the photograph wash and embossing machine (1895).

2

Mark Mallory (b. 1962), Ohio state senator and Cincinnati's mayor from 2005 to 2013.

3

Wesley Brown (b. Baltimore, Maryland, 1927), US Navy Academy's first black graduate (1949).

4

Caracalla (b. 188), twenty-second Roman emperor (198–217), fourth of African heritage; elder son of Septimius Severus, of the Severan Dynasty.

Maya Angelou (b. 1928), author and poet; wrote poem for President Bill Clinton's inauguration in 1993.

William Cowan (b. Yadkinville, North Carolina, 1969), appointed by Massachusetts governor as interim US senator (2013).

5

Booker T. Washington (b. Hale's Ford, Virginia, 1856), former slave, reformer; he wrote nine books, the best known of which is *Up from Slavery* (1901).

Colin Powell (b. New York City, 1937), Chief of Staff, Armed Forces and the US Secretary of State (2001–2005); his parents were Jamaican immigrants.

6

James A. Healy (b. Macon, Georgia, 1830), first US black Roman Catholic priest (1854) and bishop (1875).

William Cardoza (b. 1905), physician, pioneering researcher of sickle cell anemia.

7

El Greco (d. 1425), Cretan-born Spanish Renaissance painter; Of Minoan (Egyptian), Cretan, and Greek heritage.

Robert Browning (b. 1812), famed English poet and playwright; husband of Elizabeth Browning; had a Jamaican grandmother.

Allen Allensworth (b. 1842), escaped Kentucky slave, military leader, founder of Allensworth, California.

8

Robert L. Johnson (b. Hictory, Mississippi, 1946), founder of Black Entertainment Television (BET), first black billionaire (2000).

9

Paul Robeson (b. Princeton, New Jersey 1898), stellar athlete, singer, actor, and human rights activist.

10

Juan Williams (b. 1954), Panamanian American political analyst and journalist.

11

Septimius Severus (b. 165), twenty-first emperor of Rome (193–211), third of black ancestry; one of the most powerful African rulers in history; founder of the black Severan Dynasty.

Percy Julian (b. 1899), chemist who developed tests for birth control and held 130 patents.

12

Horace Cayton, Jr. (b. 1903), educator and author; wrote *The Black Metropolis.*

13

Lucy Laney (b. 1833), educator and founder of Haines Institute, Augusta, Georgia (1854).

14

Flournoy Miller (b. 1887), comedian who wrote the *Amos and Andy* radio series.

15

Leon Washington (b. Kansas City, Kansas, 1907), founding publisher of *Los Angeles Sentinel Newspaper* (1933).

Harold Washington (b. 1922), mayor of Chicago, Illinois (1983–1987).

16

Isaac Murphy (b. 1861), great Hall of Fame jockey; three-time Kentucky Derby winner.

Augustus Jackson (b. 1868), former White House chef and confectioner; dubbed the "father of ice cream."

Peter Ustinov (b. 1921), notable British-born actor; honoree of Oscar, Grammy, and Golden Globe Awards. His paternal descendants were of Russian, Polish, German, and Ethiopian descent.

17

Anicetus (d. 166), saint; eleventh pope of Roman empire (155–166), second of African lineage (Hamitic Syrian)

18

George Shirley (b. Indianapolis, Indiana, 1934), famed operatic tenor; sang more than eighty roles in five languages.

19

Pierre Landry (b. 1841), celebrated as the first US mayor of African blood (Donaldsonville, Louisiana, 1868).

20

E. Frederic Morrow (b. 1909), President Eisenhower's White House staff advisor.

21

George Washington Bush (b. Pennsylvania, 1790), Washington State trailblazer in the 1840s; founder of the city Centralia.

22

Henry Sampson (b. 1930), Mississippian physician and inventor of the gamma electric cellular phone (1971).

23

Granville Woods (b. Columbus, Ohio, 1856), inventor of the telephone transmitter; held over fifty patents.

24

Kevin Powell (b. Jersey City, New Jersey, 1966), poet, writer, entrepreneur.

25

Ella Fitzgerald (b. Newport News, Virginia, 1918), innovative jazz singer; first black woman to garner a Grammy Award (1958).

26

John Audubon (b. 1785), famed Haitian-born ornithologist, naturalist, and painter.

James Beckwourth (b. Virginia, 1789), explorer of the Sierra Nevada Mountains' California Pass, which was named in his honor.

Donald Cotton (b. 1928), invented propellants for nuclear reactors.

27

Coretta Scott King (b. Marion, Alabama, 1927), civil rights activist; widow of Martin Luther King Jr.

Cory Booker (b. Washington, DC, 1969), Rhodes Scholar, mayor of Newark; became US Senator from New Jersey (2013).

28

James Washington (b. Knoxville, Tennessee, 1948), Yale and Princeton scholar; expert on black religious history.

29

Edward "Duke" Ellington (b. Washington, DC, 1899), notable bandleader and composer.

30

Carl XVI Gustaf (b. 1946), crowned king of Sweden (1973); descendant of Charlotte Sophia.

Septimus Severus

May

"Be peaceful, be courteous, obey the law, respect everyone; but if someone puts his hands on you, send him to the cemetery."

- Macolm X

1

James Durham (b. 1762), considered to be the first black licensed physician in America (1788).

2

Elijah McCoy (b. Canada 1843), innovative inventor; known as the "Real McCoy"; held over fifty patents.

3

Alexander V (d. 1410), Roman Church antipope[5] (1409–1410); sixth and the last pope of Cretan, Greek and Egyptian stock.

4

Hosni Mubarak (b. 1928), Egyptian president (1981–2011).

5

Pio Pico (b. 1801), last California governor under Mexican rule (1832, 1845).

---

[5] Antipope: a rival pope elected in opposition to one who has been chosen by Church law.

6

John Van Salee (b. Massachusetts, 1825), first African American surgeon; served in the Civil War; descendant and son of Abraham Van Salee.

7

Mary Mahoney (b. 1845), first African American registered nurse (1879).

8

John Burris (b. Vallejo, California, 1945), esteemed civil rights defense attorney.

9

William Davis (b. New York, 1853), former Buffalo soldier; invented the modern horse riding saddle (1896).

10

P. B. S. Pinchback (b. 1837), first person of African descent to become US state governor, (Louisiana) from 1872 to 1873.
Shelby Davidson (b. 1868), notable lawyer and adding machine inventor (1908).

11

Ira Aldridge (b. New York City, 1804), legendary Shakespearian actor.
Louis Farrakhan (b. New York City, 1933), leader of the Nation of Islam since 1978.

12

Mervyn Dymally (b. 1926), Trinidadian-born California congressman and lieutenant governor.

13

John VI (b. 1767), king of Portugal and Brazil (1816–1826); parents were of Portuguese and African lineage.

Joe Louis (b. Lexington, Alabama, 1914), one of the greatest boxing champions of all time (1937–1949).

14

Archibald Alexander (b. Ottumwa, Iowa 1888), noted engineer; designed the Tidal Basin Bridge and Whitehurst Freeway.
John Rice (b. Starkville, Mississippi, 1939), clergyman, devotional poet.

15

Alvin Poussaint (b. New York City, 1934), esteemed Haitian-American psychiatrist and author.

16

John Conyers, Jr. (b. 1929), Michigan congressman and founder of the Congressional Black Caucus (1969).

17

Frederick Jones (b. Cincinnati, Ohio, 1893), prolific inventor of over sixty patents, the best known of which are the refrigerated truck systems (used to transfer food and blood during World War II) and the portable X-ray machine.

18

Alexander Miles (b. 1838), inventor of an improved elevator (1887).
Nicholas II (b. 1868), last czar of Russia (1894–1917). Descendant of Charlotte Sophia and grandson of Victoria.

19

Charlotte Sophia (b. Germany 1744), queen of King George III, Great Britain and Ireland (1761–1818); ancestress of royal and noble families across Europe.[6]

---

[6] Charlotte Sophia: A lineal descendant of Madragana, the black mistress of King Afonso III of Portugal (1440). The city of Charlotte, North Carolina, is named in her honor.

Malcolm X (b. Omaha, Nebraska, 1925), Muslim activist; founded Organization for Afro-American Unity (1964).

20

Toussaint L'Ouverture (b. 1743), Haitian liberator.

Bernardino Rivadavia (b. 1780), first president of the Argentine Republic (1826–1827).

David Paterson (b. Brooklyn, New York, 1954), first African American governor of New York (2008–2010).

21

James Gunther (b. 1932), Lutheran theologian, humanitarian, and Harlem pastor.

Loretta Lynch (b. Greensboro, North Carolina, 1959), noted lawyer; succeeded Eric Holder as US attorney general in 2015.

22

Naomi Campbell (b. 1970), London-born supermodel, actress, and entrepreneur.

23

Charles Nash (b. 1844), post–Civil War congressman from Louisiana (1875–1877).

24

Oliver Cromwell (b. 1752), Revolutionary War soldier and patriot.

Victoria (b. 1819), British queen (1837–1901) who was penned the "grandmother of Europe"; granddaughter of Queen Charlotte Sophia.

25

Bill "Bojangles" Robinson (b. Richmond, Virginia, 1878), iconic vaudeville and motion picture performer.

26

Pescennius Niger (d. 194), usurper; one of the five emperors ruling Rome in 193–194.

27

Cornelius Vanderbilt (b. Staten Island, New York, 1794), financier, philanthropist, and patriarch of the Vanderbilt clan, one of the wealthiest families of the nineteenth century; founded Vanderbilt University in 1873; great grandson of Abraham Van Salee.

28

Betty Shabazz (b. Detroit, Michigan, 1936), educator; widow of Malcolm X.

29

Eugene Marino (b. Mississippi, 1934), first black US Roman Catholic archbishop, serving in Atlanta, Georgia (1988).

30

Stepin Fetchit (b. Key West, Florida, 1902), Filmdom's premier comedic actor appeared in fifty-four films from the 1920s to the 1970s; first black millionaire entertainer.

31

Dave Roberts (b. Okinawa, Japan, 1972), first African American manager of the Los Angeles Dodgers franchise (2015).

Charlotte Sophia

Cornelius Vanderbilt

Pio Pico

June

Why should I complain about making $7,000 dollars a week playing a maid? If I didn't, I'd be making $7 dollars a week actually being one.

—Hattie McDaniel

1

Alice Parker (b. Morristown, New Jersey, 1883), Howard University alumnus and inventor of the gas heating furnace (1919).

2

Cornel West (b. Tulsa, Oklahoma, 1953), philosopher, author, and critic.

3

Charles Drew (b. Washington, DC, 1904), physician and surgeon; founder of blood banks and blood plasma banks (1940).

Josephine Baker (b. 1906), St. Louis–born entertainer; won stardom in France.

Anderson Vanderbilt Cooper (b. New York City, 1967), television journalist and show host; descendant of Abraham Van Salee (son of Gloria Vanderbilt).

4

Samuel Gravely Jr. (b. 1922), US Navy's first African American admiral (1971).

5

Ivan Gannibal (b. 1735), Russian nobleman and general; son of Abram Gannibal.

6

Aleksander Pushkin (b. 1799), Russian writer known as the "father of Russian literature"; great grandson of Abram Gannibal.

7

Gwendolyn Brooks (b. 1917), Pulitzer Prize–winning poet.

8

Muhammad (d. 632), Arab prophet, founder of Islam (610); claimed descendant of Ishmael. Tribe: Arabian- Egyptian kindred.

9

T. D. Jakes (b. South Charleston, West Virginia, 1957), bishop, pastor of The Potter's House (a mega church), and author.

Johnny Depp (b. Owensboro, Kentucky, 1963), outstanding motion picture actor; descendant of Elizabeth Key, a former Virginian slave.

10

Hattie McDaniel (b. Wichita, Kansas, 1895), actress; first black American to win an Oscar (1940); honored with a US postage stamp in 2006.

Nick Ballard (b. Santa Monica, California, 1986), motion picture and TV actor, mentor.

11

Macrimus (d. 218), twenty-fourth emperor of Rome (217–218), sixth of African heritage; part of the Severan Dynasty.

12

Barbara Harris (b. Philadelphia, Pennsylvania, 1931), became the first female bishop of the Episcopal Church (1989).

13
Jose Paez (b. 1790), two-time Venezuelan president.

14
Antonio Maceo (b. 1845), Cuban freedom fighter and patriot.

15
Salem Poor (b. Andover, Massachusetts, 1747), ex-slave, Battle of Bunker Hill soldier, patriot.

16
Desiree Rogers (b. 1959), CEO of Johnson Publishing Company.

17
James W. Johnson (b. Jacksonville, Florida, 1871), co-authored the Black American National Anthem, *"Lift Every Voice and Sing"* (1889).

18
Robert Church (b. 1839), businessman; considered the first black American millionaire (1900).

19
Andrew Hatcher (b. 1925), President John Kennedy's press secretary.
Paula Abdul (b. San Fernando, California, 1962), Grammy Award–winning singer and TV personality; her father, Harold Abdul, was of Musta Arabi and Hamitic Jewish background.

20
Lloyd Hall (b. 1894), food chemist, pioneer in food preservation.
Andre Watts (b. Germany 1946), classical pianist.

21
Joseph Rainey (b. 1832), first black American in US Congress, for South Carolina (1870–1879).

Henry O. Tanner (b. Pittsburgh, Pennsylvania, 1859), painter who achieved fame in France.

22
Katherine Dunham (b. 1909), dancer and choreographer.

23
Caesarion (b. 47 BC), Last pharaoh of Egypt (44–30 BC); son of Cleopatra and Julius Caesar.

24
Peter Salem (b. Framingham, Massachusetts, 1750), American Revolutionary hero; fought at the Battle of Saratoga (1777).

25
James Meredith (b. 1933), first African American to attend the University of Mississippi (1962).

26
Derek Jeter (b. Pequannock, New Jersey, 1974), iconic New York Yankees baseball player.

27
Paul L. Dunbar (b. 1871), poet and lyricist for *In Dahomey,* the first all-black Broadway musical (1903).
Ronald Kirk (b. 1954), first African American mayor of Dallas, Texas (1995–2002).

28
Pierre Laval (b. 1883), twice the prime minister of France (1931, 1944); of French and African heritage.

29
James Van Der Zee (b. 1886), world-acclaimed Harlem photographer.
Michael Nutter (b. 1957), elected mayor of Philadelphia, Pennsylvania (2007).

30

Lena Horne (b. Brooklyn, New York, 1917), legendary singer and actress; refused stereotypical Negro roles in the 1940s.

Paul Laurence Dunbar

Lena Horne

July

I'm so proud to have this big mouth and this curly hair, because it is African.

—Hugo Chavez

1

Benjamin Davis Sr. (b. Washington, DC, 1880), first African American general of the US Army (1940).

Wally Amos (b. Tallahassee, Florida, 1936), created the Famous Amos cookie brand; as a talent agent, discovered folk rock duo Simon and Garfunkel.

2

Eugene Chen (b. 1878), Trinidadian-born foreign minister of China (1922–1927).

Thurgood Marshall (b. Baltimore, Maryland, 1908), NAACP lawyer selected by President Johnson to be the first African American US Supreme Court justice (1967–1991).

3

Ruth Simmons (b. Grapeland, Texas, 1945), president of Brown University, Connecticut (2001–2012); the first female head of an Ivy League institution.

4

Bass Reeves (b. Arkansas, 1838), Wild West deputy, US marshal; captured over three thousand outlaws; was the "real Lone Ranger."

5

R. C. Buford (b. 1960), general manager, San Antonio Spurs basketball franchise (2002).

6

Benjamin Bradley (b. 1835), Maryland slave; developed the first steam-powered warship in 1856.

Clemmie Pennington (b. Kansas City, Missouri, 1938), popular vocalist.

7

Leroy "Satchel" Paige (b. 1904), pioneer and Baseball Hall of Fame pitcher.

8

Billy Eckstine (b. Pittsburgh, Pennsylvania, 1914), popular balladeer from the 1940s to 1980s; signature song was "I Apologize."

9

Marie Selika (b. 1849), soprano; first black entertainer to perform at the White House (1878).

DeRay McKesson (b. Baltimore, Maryland, 1985), Black Lives Matter leader, activist.

10

Mary McLeod Bethune (b. Mayesville, South Carolina, 1875), educator, White House advisor.

David Dinkins (b. Trenton, New Jersey), New York City's first African American mayor (1990–1993).

Arthur Ashe (b. Richmond, Virginia, 1943), tennis great who won three Grand Slam titles.

11

Mattiwilda Dobbs (b. Atlanta, Georgia, 1925), opera songstress who gained stardom in Sweden and Italy.

12

Emmitt McHenry (b. Forrest City, Arkansas, 1943), founded Network Solution in 1979, creating the Internet domain registries.com/.net/.org/.gov.

13

Robert Nix Jr. (b. 1928), Chief Justice of Pennsylvania Supreme Court, 1984 to 1996.

14

Maulana Karenga (b. Parsonsburg Maryland, 1941), scholar who created the Kwanzaa holiday in 1966.

Robin Szolkowy (b. 1979), German Olympic and world figure skating champion between 2001 and 2014.

15

Maggie Walker (b. 1867), entrepreneur and first American woman to form a bank (1902).

John Moon (b. 1938), co-designer of the floppy disks and disk drives for computers (Apple Inc).

16

Ida Wells Brown (b. 1867), anti-lynching crusader and co-founder of the NAACP.

17

Thomas Carter (b. 1953), Austin, Texas–born actor and filmmaker.

Gary Gray (b. New York City, 1968), film director, *Straight Outta Compton* (2015).

18

Nelson Mandela (b. 1918), South African patriot and the nation's first black president (1994–1999).

19

Walter Turnbull (b. 1944), founding director, Boys Choir of Harlem (1975).

20

Leonidas Berry (b. Woodsdale North Carolina, 1902), biopsy gastro scope inventor; president, National Medical Association (1965).

21

Jim Clyburn (b. 1940), South Carolina Human Affairs Commissioner elected to US Congress in 1993.

22

Alessandro de Medici (b. 1510), first Duke of Florence (Italy); son of Pope Clement VII.

23

Haile Sellassie (b. 1891), legendary Ethiopian emperor (1930–1974); Rastafarians revered him as the Messiah of the Bible.

24

Simon Bolivar (b. Venezuela, 1783), great South American revolutionary soldier and liberator; mother was of Canarian (African) descent.
Alexandre Dumas the Elder (b. 1802), French novelist of *The Three Musketeers* and *The Count of Monte Cristo.*
George T. Sampson: (b. 1861), inventor of the sled propeller (1885) and the clothes dry-cleaning processer (1892).

25

Emmitt Till (b. 1941), fourteen-year-old from Chicago who was lynched in Money, Mississippi, in 1955.

26

Dorothea Towles (b. Texarkana, Texas, 1922), first black professional fashion model (Paris, 1945); designer, Christian Dior.

27

Alexandre Dumas the Younger (b. 1824), French playwright.

28

Victor I (d. 199), saint; fourteenth Roman pope (189–199), third of African descent; established Latin as language of the Church; started the celebration of Easter on Sundays.

Jacqueline Bouvier Kennedy (b. Southampton, New York), First Lady and wife of President John F. Kennedy; descendant of Alexander Van Salee.

Hugo Chavez (b. 1954), president of Venezuela (1999–2013); had Spanish, Indian, and African parentage.

29

Chester Himes (b. 1909), wrote detective novels set in Harlem, such as *Cotton Comes to Harlem*.

30

Anita Hill (b. Lone Tree, Oklahoma, 1956), Yale academic and attorney.

Clementa Pinckney (b. 1973), South Carolina state senator, A. M. E. pastor, martyr.

31

Evonne Goolagong (b. 1951), Australian tennis champion.

Deval Patrick (b. Chicago, Illinois, 1956), first black Massachusetts governor, elected in 2006 and re-elected in 2010.

Pope Victor I

Simon Bolivar

August

There are no warlike people, just warlike leaders.

—Ralph Bunche

1

Helvius Pertinax (b. 126), son of an ex-slave; became the nineteenth Roman emperor (193), the first of black ancestry.

2

James Baldwin (b. Harlem, New York, 1924), playwright of the drama *Blues for Mister Charlie* (1964), based on the lynching of Emmitt Till.

3

Roland Burris (b. 1937), US senator from Chicago, Illinois (2009–2010).

4

Louis Armstrong (b. New Orleans, Louisiana 1901), pioneer jazz musician who created the scatting style.

Barack Obama (b. Hawaii, 1961), forty-fourth US president, *second of African descent.*

Keith Ellison (b. 1963), first Muslim elected to US Congress (1907), from Minnesota.

5

Bill Richmond (Staten Island, New York, 1763), known as the "Black Terror," in 1804 he became the first US black professional boxer.

Charles E. Blake (b. Little Rock, Arkansas 1940), Pentecostal COGIC theologian and bishop.

6

Bennett Stewart (b. 1912): Illinois Congressman (1979–1981).

7

Ralph Bunche (b. Detroit, Michigan, 1904), diplomat, co-founder of the United Nations (1944).

8

Matthew Henson (b. Nanjemoy, Maryland, 1886), explorer of the North Pole (1919), accompanied Robert Peary.

9

Anne Brown (b. 1912), soprano; created the role of Bess in folk-opera *Porgy and Bess*.

10

Afonso (b. 1377), first Duke of Braganza (1442–1461); forebear of Portuguese and Brazilian monarchs; son of John I, king of Portugal, and Ines Pires, his black secondary wife.

Vicente Guerrero (b. 1782), second president of Mexico (1829).

11

Alex Haley (b. Ithaca, New York, 1921), authored the novel *Roots: The Saga of an American Family* (1970).

12

Cleopatra VII (d. 30 BC), world's most celebrated queen; reigned in Egypt from 51 to 30 BC. Descendant of Queen Laodice (of Greek, Anatolian and Afro- Persian blood)

George IV (b. 1762), king of Great Britain and the British Empire (1820–1830); son of Queen Charlotte Sophia.

Luis Sanchez (b. 1889), president of Peru (1931–1933).

13

Joycelyn Elders (b. 1933), pediatrician; America's first black surgeon general (1993–1994).

14

Earvin "Magic" Johnson (b. Lansing, Michigan, 1959), Former Lakers superstar, millionaire entrepreneur.

Halle Berry (b. Cleveland, Ohio, 1968), first African American Best Actress Oscar winner (2002).

15

Biddy Mason (b. 1818), early California landlord and philanthropist; claimed she walked from Georgia to California; a founder of the First A. M. E. Church in Los Angeles, California.

16

Carol Moseley-Braun (b. Chicago, Illinois, 1947), first black female US Senator (1993–1999).

17

Menelik II (b. 1844), Ethiopian emperor (1889–1913); proclaimed to be a descendant of King Solomon and the queen of Sheba (of the Bible).

Marcus Garvey (b. Jamaica, 1887), leader of the Black Nationalist movement during the 1920s.

18

Denmark Vesey (b. Virgin Islands, 1767), slave insurrectionist; founder of Charleston, South Carolina, Emanuel A. M. E. Church (1818).

19

Charles Bolden (b. 1946), astronaut; piloted space shuttles *Columbia* (1986) and *Discovery* (1990).

20

Twenty Africans arrived in America as indentured servants at Jamestown, Virginia, 1619.

DeForest Soaries (b. 1951), New Jersey Secretary of State (1999).

21

Count Basie (b. Red Bank, New Jersey, 1906), legendary jazz musician and composer.

22

Juan de Pareja (d. 1670), enslaved servant who became one of Spain's greatest painters.

23

Marshall Sharpe (b. Plainfield, New Jersey, 1949), C. M. E. pastor and human rights advocate.

Chelsi Smith (b. Redwood City, California, 1973), pageant queen; first black Miss Texas, Miss USA, and Miss Universe (1995).

Kobe Bryant (b. Philadelphia, Pennsylvania, 1978), five-time NBA champion, played from 1996 to 2016.

24

Philip Downing (b. 1850), invented the US postal mail box (1891).

25

Althea Gibson (b. Silver, South Carolina, 1927), tennis champion.

26

Hale Woodruff (b. 1900), renowned print master.

27

Jennifer Carroll (b. Trinidad, 1959), Florida lieutenant governor (2011–2013).

28

Rita Dove (b. Akron, Ohio, 1952), US Poet Laureate (1993–1995).

29

Joseph Winters (b. 1824), Virginian slave, invented the fire escape ladder (1878).

Otis Boykin (b. Dallas, Texas, 1920), inventor of the guided missile resistor and pacemaker control unit.

30

Joseph Howze (b. 1923), Roman Catholic bishop, Diocese of Biloxi, Mississippi (1977–2001).

31

Charles Gittens (b. 1928), first African American Secret Service agent (1956); served in North Carolina, New York, and Puerto Rico.

Frank Robinson (b. Beaumont, Texas, 1935), professional baseball player and first black manager of a major baseball league, with the Cleveland Indians (1974–1977).

Emperor Pertinax

Louis Armstrong

Barack Hussein Obama

September

Knowledge is the key that unlocks all doors. It doesn't matter what you look like or where you come from if you have knowledge.

—Benjamin Carter

1

Estevancio (d. 1539), African explorer from Mexico; led the expedition that discovered Arizona and New Mexico in 1534.

2

Romare Bearden (b. 1912), celebrated modernist artist from Charlotte, North Carolina.

3

Rufus Stokes (b. 1922), inventor of an antipollution device, Air Exhaust Purifier (1968).

4

Lewis Latimer (b. 1848), a draftsman from Chelsea, Massachusetts; inventor of the electric lamp (1874).

Richard Wright (b. 1908), best-selling writer of *Native Son* and *Black Boy*.

5

Frank Yerby (b. Augusta, Georgia, 1916), prolific writer; three of his novels were adapted for movies: *The Foxes of Harrow* (1947), *The Golden Hawk* (1952), *Saracen Blade* (1954).

6

Joel Rogers (b. Jamaica, 1883), Afrocentric historian and researcher.
Michaelle Jean (b. Haiti, 1957), governor-general of Canada (2005–2010).

7

Jean Hutson (b. 1914), curator, Schomburg Center for Research Black Culture.

8

Charles H. Mason (b. 1847), religious leader and founder, Church of God in Christ (1895).

9

Philippus Arabs (d. 249), reigned as the thirty-third Roman emperor (244–249), the ninth of African roots.

10

Misty Copeland (b. Kansas City, Missouri, 1982), ballerina; elevated to be principal dancer of American Ballet Theatre in 2015.

11

Charles Evers (b. 1922), Mississippian civil righter and the first black mayor of Fayette, Mississippi (1969).
Jeh Johnson (b. 1957), President Obama's US Secretary of Homeland Security (2013).

12

Prince Hall (b. 1748), ex-slave in Boston; created the first Masonic lodge for blacks (1797).

Jesse Owens (b. Oakville, Alabama, 1913), track and field great; won four gold medals at Hitler's 1937 Olympic games, held in Berlin, Germany.

13

Alain Locke (b. Philadelphia, Pennsylvania, 1885), Harvard alumnus and the first black Rhodes Scholar (1907).

Tyler Perry (b. New Orleans, Louisiana, 1969), acclaimed actor, playwright, and film producer.

14

Constance Motley (b. 1921), first African American woman federal judge (1966).

15

Jan Matzeliger (b. Suriname, South America, 1852), inventor of the machine that made an entire shoe (1883) and revolutionized the shoe industry; was of African and Dutch heritage.

George Grant (b. 1847), Boston dentist and the inventor of the golf tee (1899).

16

Cyprian (d. 258), saint, bishop of Carthage (Africa), early Christian writer, and martyr.

17

Andrew "Rube" Foster (b. 1879), pioneer Baseball Hall of Fame pitcher and manager.

18

Benjamin Carson (b. Detroit, Michigan, 1951), neurosurgeon; first to successfully separate Siamese twins (1987).

19

Tim Scott (b. 1965), first African American senator from the state of South Carolina (2013).

Soledad O'Brien (b. St. James, New York, 1966), Emmy Award–winning television journalist; (African Cuban mother).

20
Abram Gannibal (b. Ethiopia, 1696), African slave kidnapped at age seven; became chief general of the Russian army.

21
Kwame Nkrumah (b. 1909), Ghana's first president (1957–1966).

22
Maurice (d. 287), African soldier; patron saint of Germany and Switzerland; martyr.
Lee Burridge (b. Paris, France, 1861), typewriter inventor (1884).

23
Linus (d. 76), saint; successor to St. Peter as second Roman pope (67–76), the first of African (Mauritanian)descent.

24
Herb Jeffries (b. Detroit, Michigan, 1913), singer and actor in all-black western films of the 1940s; died at age one hundred.

25
John I Phokas, emperor of the Byzantine (Eastern) Roman Empire (969–976), the twelfth of black heritage; nephew of Emperor Nicephorus II.

26
John Lee Love (b. Fall River, Massachusetts, 1870), carpenter, inventor of the pencil sharper (1897).
Richard Horton (b. Augusta, Georgia 1938), prominent clergyman and a religious critic.

27

Hiram Revels (b. (Fayette, North Carolina, 1827), ex-barber and preacher; America's first senator of African descent (1870–1871), from Mississippi.

28

Richard Harrison (b. Ontario, Canada, 1864), distinguished stage actor.

29

Nelson Trout (b. Columbus, Ohio, 1920), second black bishop of the Lutheran Church (1983).

Charles Cooper (b. Pittsburgh, Pennsylvania, 1926), the National Basketball Association's first signed black player (1950).

30

Jose M. Morelos (b. 1765), Mexican priest and patriot.

Johnny Mathis (b. Gilmer, Texas, 1935), popular singer over four decades.

Lewis Latimer

Jesse Owens

October

I am sick and tired of being sick and tired.

—Fanny Lou Hamer

1

Severus Alexander (b. 208), twenty-sixth emperor of Rome (222–235), the eighth of black lineage; part of the Severan Dynasty.

George Carruthers (b. Cincinnati, Ohio, 1939), premier inventor of the radiator detector (1969) and the first moon-based space observatory (1972).

2

Nat Turner (b. 1800), slave, preacher, and freedom fighter; led the greatest slave rebellion in the US history in Southampton, Virginia (1831).

Nilo Pecanha (b. 1867), president of Brazil (1900–1901).

Johnnie Cochran Jr. (b. Shreveport, Louisiana, 1937), high-profile defense attorney.

3

Chubby Checker (b. 1941), rock and roll singer; best known as creator of the dance craze the Twist (1960).

4

Russell Simmons (b. New York City, 1957), recording executive and pioneer producer in the hip-hop industry.

5

Benjamin Reid (b. 1937), bishop, Church of God (1972–1996); Inglewood, California, pastor.

Yvonne Brathwaite-Burke (b. 1932), former congresswoman; Los Angeles County supervisor.

6

Fannie Lou Hamer (b. 1917), founder of the Mississippi Freedom Democratic Party (1964).

Lonnie Johnson (b. Mobile, Alabama 1949), invented the Super Soaker water gun (1982), the world's top toy.

7

Elijah Muhammad (b. 1897), Muslim leader who proposed a separate state for black Americans in 1960.

8

Earl Ofari Hutchinson (b. 1966), journalist who authored a dozen books related to black American diaspora.

9

David Cameron (b. 1966), elected prime minister of Great Britain in 2010; descendant of Charlotte Sophia.

Steven McQueen (b. London, England, 1969), Oscar-winning film producer of *12 Years a Slave,* 2013,

10

Theolonious Monk (b. Rocky Mount, North Carolina, 1917), developer of bebop jazz.

Hazel Johnson (b. West Chester, Pennsylvania, 1927), first African American woman general (1979).

11

R. Nathaniel Dett (b. 1882), composer of Negro spirituals and folksongs.

12

Dorie Miller (b. Waco, Texas, 1919), sailor and hero during Pearl Harbor attack in 1941; awarded the Navy Cross.

13

Jesse Brown (b. 1926), first African American naval aviator (1948).

14

Cornell Brooks (b. El Paso, Texas, 1961), CEO and president of NAACP (2014).

15

Fanny Coppin (b. 1837), missionary, educator; Coppin State University in Baltimore, Maryland, is named in her honor.

16

Ebenezer Bassett (b. 1833), first African American diplomat; served as ambassador to Haiti (1869).

17

Mae Carol Jemison (b. Decatur, Alabama, 1956), physician and first black female astronaut (1987).

18

Brenda Lawrence (b. 1954), US congresswoman representing Michigan (2014).

19

Michael Steele (b. Andrews Field, Maryland, 1958), Maryland's lieutenant governor (2003–2007); Republican analyst.

20

Jomo Kenyatta (b. 1891), founding father of the Kenyan nation (1963).

Kamala Harris (b. Oakland, California, 1964), elected as attorney general of California (2010, 2014), US Senator (2016).

21

Jim Hill (b. San Antonio, Texas, 1946), top-tier television sportscaster.

Ronald McNair (b. Lake City, South Carolina, 1950), astronaut; died in the *Challenger* space shuttle explosion in 1986.

22

Aemilianus (d. 253), African-born thirty-ninth emperor of Rome (253), the tenth of black ancestry.

Lewis Temple (b. 1800), Virginian slave, as a blacksmith, he invented the standard harpoon used in the whaling industry (1848).

James Bland (b. 1854), composer of some seven hundred songs, including Virginia's state song "Carry Me Back to Old Virginny."

23

Pele (b. 1940), Brazilian athlete; considered the world's greatest soccer player.

Kevin Krigger (b. Virgin Islands 1983), Kentucky Derby jockey.

24

Rafael Carrera (b. 1814), Guatemala liberator and president (1844).

25

William B. Purvis (b. Philadelphia, Pennsylvania. 1851), inventor of fountain pen (1890), the paper bag machine, and the self-inking hand stamp.

Emmett Chappelle (b. 1925), biochemist; discovered techniques to detect bacteria in blood and food (1966).

26

Edward Brooke (b. 1919), Massachusetts Republican; state attorney general (1963–1967); first black US senator since Reconstruction (1967–1979).

27

Valerie Thomas (b. 1943), Maryland scientist and inventor of the illusion transmitter (1980).

28

Willis Johnson (b. Cincinnati, Ohio, 1857), inventor of the mechanical egg beater (1884).

29

Ellen J. Sirleaf (b. 1938), Africa's first female president, of Liberia (2006).

30

Marie Brown (b. 1922), Native New Yorker, native who invented the home security system (1969).

Samuel Kountz (b. Lexa, Arkansas, 1930), celebrated surgeon and a pioneer in kidney transplantation surgery.

31

Carlos Mendoza (b. 1856), president of Panama (1910).

Ethel Waters (b. Chester, Pennsylvania, 1896), acclaimed stage and film actress; starred in film classics *Cabin in the Sky* (1943) and *Pinky* (1949).

St. Gelasius I

Nilo Pecanha

November

The world is a book, and those who do not travel read only a page.

—St. Augustine

1

Barry C. Black (b. Baltimore, Maryland, 1948), first African American US Senate chaplain (2003).

2

Warren G. Harding (b. 1865), Ohio Republican who was elected the twenty-ninth US president (1921–1923). He was the "first" president of African extraction, as a descendant of Abraham Van Salee.

Richard Spikes (b. San Francisco, California, 1884), Distinguished inventor: automatic car washer 1913; automatic gear shift, 1932.

3

Louis Sullivan (b. 1933), founder of the Morehouse School of Medicine, Atlanta, (1978).

4

Buddy Bolden (b. 1868), formed the first jazz band in the 1890s.

Patricia Bath (b. New York City, 1942), physician and inventor of the Laser-phaco that removes eye cataracts (1986).

5

George Crum (b. Malta, New York, 1822), inventor of one of the world's most famous snacks, the potato chip (1853).

6

George Poage (b. 1880), first African American Olympic medalist, in track and field (1904).

Juanita Hall (b. 1901), first black actress to win a Tony Award, for *South Pacific* (1950).

7

George Gibbs (b. 1916), explorer of the South Pole (Antarctica); accompanied Richard Byrd in 1939.

Joaquin Hendricks-Diaz (b. 1951), governor of the Mexican state Quintana Roo (1999–2005).

8

Firmus (d. 375), third and last black Roman usurper; ruled the Africa Province in 375.

9

Benjamin Banneker (b. 1731), scientist, astronomer, and co-planner of Washington, DC, in 1791.

Dorothy Dandridge (b. Cleveland, Ohio, 1922), singer, actress, and Oscar nominee for the 1954 film *Carmen Jones*.

10

Michael Lee-Chin (b. 1951), Jamaican-born billionaire, philanthropist.

11

E. V. Hill (b. 1933), influential Los Angeles minister and President Richard Nixon's advisor.

12

Diane Watson (b. 1933), US Congresswoman from California, serving from 2003 to 2011.

13

Augustine of Hippo (b. 354), saint; African bishop deemed as the "father of Christian theology." St. Augustine, Florida, the oldest city in America (1565), was named in his honor.

14

Condoleezza Rice (b. Birmingham, Alabama, 1954), US Secretary of State (2005–2009).

Valerie Jarrett (b. Iran, 1956), President Barack Obama's senior advisor (2015).

15

Sarah Woodson (b. 1825), first black women's college instructor, at Wilberforce University (1858).

16

William C. Handy (b. Florence, Alabama, 1874), composer who's called "father of the blues."

17

William Hastie (b. 1904), first black US federal judge (1937); governor of the Virgin Islands (1946).

18

William Wells Brown (b. Kentucky, 1815), former slave and the United States' first black novelist, penning *Clotel* (1853).

J. C. Watts (b. 1957), Oklahoma's sole African American elected to the US Congress (1999–2003).

19

Roy Campanella (b. Philadelphia, Pennsylvania, 1921), Brooklyn Dodgers Hall of Fame catcher.

20

Charles Gilpin (b. 1878), vaudeville and stage actor.

21

Gelasius (d. 496), saint; forty-ninth pope of Rome (492–496), fifth of African descent.

Angelo Soliman (d. 1796), African-born Free Masonic pioneer and classical composer; Mozart composed his opera *The Magic Flute* in his honor.

22

Guion Bluford Jr. (b. Philadelphia, Pennsylvania, 1942), first African American astronaut in space (1983).

23

Emmett Ashford (b. 1916), first black American Major League Baseball umpire (1965).

24

Scott Joplin (b. 1868), composer and originator of ragtime music.

Robert Sengstacke (b. 1870), publisher of the newspaper *Chicago Defender* (1905).

25

Joe Gans (b. 1874), legendary boxing champion of the early 1900s.

26

Abu-al-Quasim (d. 1013), African Spaniard, Middle Ages physician; called the "father of modern surgery."

27

J. Ernest Wilkins, Jr. (b. 1923), nuclear scientist; co-developer of the atom bomb (1944).

Caroline Kennedy (b. New York City, 1957), lawyer, diplomat, and daughter of John and Jacqueline Kennedy; a descendant of Abraham Van Salee.

28

Berry Gordy Jr. (b. Detroit, Michigan, 1929), established Motown Records Corp. with a family $800 loan in 1959.

29

Adam C. Powell Jr. (b. 1908), charismatic Harlem clergyman and congressman (1945–1971).

30

George Cook (b. Kentucky, 1857), inventor of the automatic fishing device in 1899.

Shirley Chisholm (b. 1924), the first African American woman elected to Congress (1969).

Joe Gans

Warren G. Harding

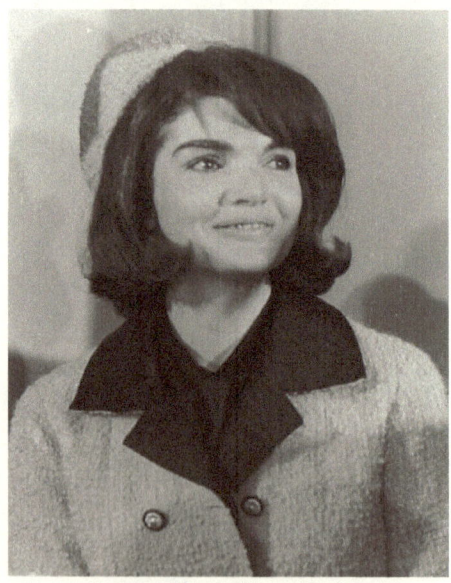

Jacqueline Kennedy

December

Luck is when an opportunity comes along and you're prepared for it.

—Denzel Washington

1

Kurt Schmoke (b. 1949), first African American mayor of Baltimore, Maryland (1987–1999).

Cheryl Boone Isaacs (b. Springfield, Massachusetts, 1949), president of the Academy Awards Association, elected in 2013.

2

Harry T. Burleigh (b. 1866), esteemed singer and composer of Negro spirituals and folksongs.

3

Jean B. Pointe DuSable (b. Haiti, 1745), frontiersman and trader; founder of the city Chicago, Illinois, in 1779.

Roderick Ireland (b. 1953), Chief Justice, Massachusetts Supreme Court (2010).

4

Tyra Banks (b. Inglewood, California. 1973), supermodel, television personality.

5

Bill Pickett (b. 1870), original Texan cowboy and rodeo showman; introduced steer wrestling; white ranchers were called cattlemen, but blacks were called cowboys.

6

Mia Love (b. Brooklyn, New York, 1975), Haitian American; first black Republican Congresswoman, of Utah (2015).

7

Carole Simpson (b. Chicago, Illinois 1941), first African American female TV journalist, in 1974.

J. Edgar Boyd (b. Florida, 1947), FAME minister and social justice advocate.

8

Sammy Davis Jr. (b. New York City, 1925), multi-talented entertainer whose career began at age six.

9

Martin dePorres (b. 1579), saint; first black priest of the western hemisphere (Peru); canonized in 1962.

10

Nicephorus II Phokas (d. 969), Byzantine Roman emperor (963–969), eleventh of African stock. His family was of Greek, Arab, Turkish, and African descent.

Nicephorus III Phokas (d. 1081), emperor, Byzantine Roman Empire (1078–1081); descendant of Nicephorus II; thirteenth and last black ruler of the Roman Empire.

11

Morris Turner (b. 1923), noted syndicated cartoonist of *Wee Pals* (1965), the first racially diverse comic strip.

12

Minnie Evans (b. 1892), artist known for her Southern folk themes.

13

Elizabeth Key (b. Virginia 1630), first African American slave to sue for freedom and win (1656).

14

John Langston (b. 1829), Virginia Reconstruction statesman in the 1890s; an Oklahoma town and university are named in his honor.

15

William Hinton (b. 1883), bacteriologist who developed the Hinton test for diagnosing syphilis (1927).

16

Henry Blair (b. Glen Ross, Maryland, 1807), second black to receive a patent for an invention, a corn planter (1834); invented the cotton planter in 1836.
Thurbert Baker (b. 1952), Georgia attorney general (1997–2011).

17

Calvin Walter (b. Baton Rouge. Louisiana, 1937), major general of the Persian Gulf War (1990–1991).

18

Benjamin Davis Jr. (b. Washington, DC, 1912), former Tuskegee Airman and US Air Force's first black general (1998).

19

Carter G. Woodson (b. New Canton, Virginia, 1875), historian; inaugurated Black History Week (1926).
Edith Piaf (b. 1915), one of France's most beloved singers, known for *La Vie en Rose*. Her maternal grandmother was of French, Italian, and African descent.

20

Franz Fanon (b. 1925), Martinique-born psychiatrist and philosopher.

21

Benjamin Disraeli (b. 1804), was twice Britain's prime minister (1868, 1874); (of Musta Arabi, Hamitic, and Jewish heritage).

Harvey Johnson (b. 1946), elected Jackson, Mississippi, mayor (2009–2013).

22

Arthur W. Mitchell (b. 1883), first black elected in Congress as a Democrat, in Illinois (1935–1943).

23

Madame C. J. Walker (b. 1867), pioneer businesswoman; first American female self-made millionaire (1921).

24

Lee Daniels (b. Philadelphia, Pennsylvania, 1959), filmmaker and producer; top credits include *Precious* (2009) and *The Butler* (2013).

25

Humphrey Bogart (b. New York City, 1899), all-time great film actor who appeared in seventy-five films (1921–1956); descendant of Abraham Van Salee.

Cab Calloway (b. Rochester, New York), singer and bandleader; consultant for 1984 movie *The Cotton Club*.

26

Jean Toomer (b. 1894), author who wrote the modernist novel *Cane* (1923).

27

Leo Africanus (d. 1554), African Spaniard who was an early geographer and historian; studied in Timbuktu, Africa.

28

Hugh MacDonald (b. 1950), rocket catapult inventor.

Denzel Washington (b. Mount Vernon, New York, 1954), accomplished actor who is a Golden Globe, Tony, and Academy Award winner.

29

Emory Malick (b. Pennsylvania 1881), America's first licensed black aviator (1912).

Thomas Bradley (b. Calvert, Texas, 1917), mayor of Los Angeles for four terms (1973–1993).

30

Eldrick "Tiger" Woods (b. Cypress, California 1975), internationally famed champion golfer.

31

Charles Ramsey (b. Chicago. Illinois, 1950), Philadelphia police commissioner (2008).

Gabrielle "Gabby" Douglas (b. Newport News, Virginia, 1995), 2012 Olympic gymnast with multiple gold medals.

**Nicephorus III with St.
Chrysostome and archangel Michael**

Nicephorus III

Humphrey Bogart

More Black Quotes

"Do not count your chicken before they hatched." —Aesop

"No one makes war on anyone, and no one steps outside his own territory. Some worship the sun ... yet others are Christians in the style of the Egyptians." —Leo Africanus, "Description of Africa," 1526.

"One's work may be finished some day; but one's education, never." — Alexandre Dumas the Elder

"It has been the fashion of Euro-American writers to deny that the Egyptians were Blacks and claim they are the same race as themselves. This has, I have no doubt, been largely due to a wish to deprive Blacks of the moral support of Ancient Greatness and to appropriate the same to the white race." —Frederick Douglass

"If the Egyptians and the majority of the tribes of northern Africa were not Blacks, then

there are no Blacks in the United States." —Carter G. Woodson

"In Russia I felt like a full human being. No color prejudice like in Mississippi, no color

prejudice like in Washington." —Paul Robeson

"People always say I didn't give my seat up because I was tired, but that isn't true. I was not tired physically. No, the only tired I was, was tired of giving in." —Rosa Parks

"Life is not a spectator sport, if you're going to spend your whole life in the grandstand just watching that goes on, in my opinion you're wasting your life." —Jackie Robinson

"Africa will write its own history, and north and south of the Sahara. It will be in history full of glory and dignity." —Patrice Lumumba

"I'm not trying to make anyone forget about Babe Ruth, I just want them to remember Henry Aaron." —Henry "Hank" Aaron

"Most people can't deal with reality, but indulge heavily in fantasy and fear. —Betty Shabazz

"Service to others is the rent you pay for your room here on earth." —Muhammad Ali

"Nothing can stand in the way of the power of millions of voices calling for change." —Barack Obama

"If you're afraid to fail, then, you're probably going to fail." —Kobe Bryant

"During slavery, we had zero unemployment." —Anonymous

Special Abbreviations

AD: Anno Domini (In the year of the Lord)

FAME: First African Methodist Episcopal

BC: Before Christ

BETL Black Entertainment Television

CEOL chief executive officer

CME: Christian Methodist Episcopal

COGIC: Church of God in Christ

NAACP: National Association for the Advancement of Colored People

NBA: National Basketball Association

PGA: Professional Golfers' Association

PhD: doctor of philosophy

UK: United Kingdom (England, Scotland, Northern Ireland, and Wales)

List of Sources

Bates, Otis. *The Eastern Libyans: An Essay.* London: United Kingdom, 1914.

Burris, Simon. *The Afro-Factor.* Inglewood, CA: H. T. Tidings, 2002.

Cooley, Williams. *The Negroland of the Arabs.* London: UK, 1841.

Du Bois, William E. D. *The Negro and Africa,* New York: International Publishers, 1915.

Evans, Arthur. *The Early Nilotic: Libyan and Egyptian Relation with Minoan Crete.* London, UK: 1925.

Gadd, K. M. *From Ur to Rome.* London, UK: Ginn and Co. Ltd., 1936.

Halley, Henry H. *Halley's Bible Handbook.* Grand Rapids, Michigan: Zondervan Publishing House, 1965.

Lindo, Hiam. *The History of the Jews of Spain and Portugal.* London, UK: Wertheimer and Company, 1848.

Public Broadcasting Service. *Frontline.* Costa Mesa, California, 2010.

Taylor, Romeo. *True Black History as It Has Never Been Told.* Las Vegas: Cable TV Advertising Concepts, Ltd.

Vernon, Patrick. *List: 100 Great Black Britons.* London: Ever Generation Publisher, 2002.

Work, Monroe. *The Negro Year Book: 1922, 1924, 1931, 1937.* Alabama: Tuskegee Institute.

Suggested Readings
and Reviews

Appiah, Kwame A., Henry L. Gates. *The Encyclopedia of the African and African American Experience.* New York: Basic Civitus Books, 1999.

Ashtor, Elishu, *The Jews of Modern Spain,* Philadelphia: Jewish Publication Society of America, 1979.

Barbosa, Ignacio. *Casa de Braganza, Memories Historia.* Lisbon, Portugal: Taylor and Francis, 1886.

Beckererath, Jurgen Von. *Chronology of the Egyptian Pharaohs.* Mainz, Germany: Philip Press, 1997.

Delancy, John J. *Dictionary of Saints.* Garden City, New York: Doubleday & Company Inc., 1980.

Gage, Betty. *Our First Black President: Warren Harding.* New York Times .(April 6, 2008)

Hyman, Mark. *Blacks Before America.* Trenton, New Jersey: Africa World Press, Inc., 1994.

Malcomson, Scott. *One Drop of Blood.* New York: Farrar Giroir, 2000.

Powers, Retha. *Barlett's Familiar Black Quotations.* Boston: Little, Brown & Co., 2013.

Rendina, Claudio. *The Pope's Histories and Secrets.* Rome: Seven Locks Press, 2002.

Rogers, J. A. *The Amazing Facts about the Negro,* New York: Futuro Press Inc., 1930.

————. *World's Greatest Men of Color.* New
York: Futuro Press Inc., 1947.

Spangeburg, Ray,Kit Moser. *African Americans in Science,
Math, and Inventions.* New York: Face on File, 2003.

Valdes y Cocum, Mario de. *Blurred Racial Lines
of the Famous.* PBS Frontline series, 1986.

Windson, Rudolph R. *From Babylon to Timbuktu.*
Jericho, New York: Exposition Press, 1969.

Bonus:

MORE Notable Persons of African Ancestry in the Bible

2500 BC TO AD 76

With complete scriptural proof

Lips that speak knowledge are a rare jewel. (Proverb . 20:15)

The earliest history of blacks or Africans, commonly known as Hamites, dates back to the Holy Bible in the book of Genesis, chapter 10. Noah's three sons, Shem ("name"), Ham ("hot, swarthy"), and Japheth ("fair"), are described as the progenitors and founders of the original seventy nations of the world.

Race as an identifying factor is not found in the Scriptures. Race, or one's ethnicity, usually was traced by and through a surname, family tree, tribal branch, clan, or national lineage.

Shem, Noah's eldest son, and his Shemite (Semitic) descendants, occupied Persia and the western Arabian peninsula. Later, they uprooted the Canaanites from their homeland, Palestine (Israel). According to the Scriptures, Abraham, the father of Judaism, was born in the town of Ur of the Chaldees (Babylonia). Thus, the Abrahams were Jewish Semites by birth, and by bloodline were of Ethnic Ethiopian stock (Gen. 10:10; Gen. 11:31).

Japheth, the second son of Noah, and his offspring (Japhethites; Europeans; Caucasians) settled in Greece and Rome, as well as throughout the European continent.

HAM (Hamites):

Ham's four sons, Ethiopia, Egypt, Libya and Canaan became the forefathers of all dark and black races of mankind. Their offspring and descendants were originally called Hamites, who populated Africa and the adjoining areas of southwest Asia collectively known as the Land of Ham (ancient Africa).

We've paraphrased the definition of who is a Hamite with who is black. A Hamite is a person with any traceable amount of black and African blood / ancestors. The word *Africa* is derived from the Roman cognomen *Afri,* a Hamitic people who dwelt in Numidia, a Roman colony located in northern Africa (200–40 BC), after which the continent of Africa was named.

The Bible text can be divided roughly into four global spheres, ranking in order of prominence: The Land of Ham, Roman, Greek, and Persian dominions. From Genesis to Revelation, the overwhelming majority of people, places, and events came "out of Africa." Let's review eight principal events.

Land of Ham

1. Garden of Eden: the birthplace of humanity. Genesis 2:8–14 (Ethiopia to Babylonia)
2. Birthplace of Abraham and Judaism. Genesis 12–16 (Ur, Chaldea/Babylonia) 2000 BC
3. Moses and the Ten Commandments. Exodus 20 (Sinia, Egypt), 1445–1446 BC
4. Samson and Delilah account. Judges 16 (Philistine), 1075 BC
5. Birthplace of David, 1040 BC; Jesus, 6 or 5 BC (Bethlehem, Israel). Christianity
6. Apostle Paul's birth, homeland. Acts 9 (Asia Minor), AD 5
7. First Gentile Christian church. Acts 11 (Antioch, Syria), AD 30
8. 8. Post-Bible epoch: Muhammad, founder of Islam (Arabia), AD 610

For the following entries, this is the format: entry or name, literal meaning in parentheses, very brief biographical sketch, two or more scriptural-based proofs of Hamitic (black) bloodline, timeline (when applicable), and the primary African progenitor.

Please note that this category is not designed to survey hundreds of entries. Nevertheless, it is a snapshot gallery that serves as a Bible reference supplement to our calendar furnished in *700 Notable Persons of African Ancestry.*

Old Testament

Ethiopia (Cush, "black"). The eldest son of Ham, the progenitor and founder of the ethnic Ethiopian nations of Ethiopia; Assyria, Babylonia, and Chaldea (Iraq); Midian and Seba (Arabia); and Nubia (Sudan), as well as the Sub-Saharan nations Kenya, Nigeria, Niger, and Liberia.

Ancestor: Ethiopia. Genesis 10:1, Chronicles 1:8–10

Egypt (Mizraim, "Land of Ham"). The second son of Ham and the founder of the country bearing his name. The forefather of the Egyptians, Arabians, Cretans (first Greeks), Edomites, and Philistines (Palestinians). Edomites were of Egyptian and Canaanite lineage.

Ancestor: Egypt. Genesis 10:1, 13–14; Genesis 21:13; 1 Chronicles 1:8, 11–16

Libya (Put, "bowman"). Ham's third son and founder of Libya, Algeria, Tunisia, Morocco and Mauritania.

Ancestor: Libya. Genesis 10:6; 1 Chronicles 1:8; Nahum 3:9

Canaan ("low"). The fourth and youngest son of Ham; ancestor of the family of Canaanites. Canaan had eleven sons, and the most mentioned in the Scriptures were Sidon (Sidonians/Phoenicians) and Jebus (Jebusites). With the Hivites, Amorites, and Heth, the father of the Hittites, their homeland was Asia-Minor, in present-day Turkey. Jesus and David had Canaanite ancestors.

Ancestor: Canaan. Genesis 10:6–19; 1 Chronicles 1:8, 13–16

Nimrod ("mighty"). The oldest son of Ethiopia, a mighty hunter, and the world's first great conqueror. He was the founder of Mesopotamian empires of Assyria, Babylonia, and Chaldea (Iraq). The prophet Micah identified Assyria as "the land of Nimrod."

Ancestor: Ethiopia. Genesis 10:8–12; Micah 5:6

Sidon ("fortress"). Canaan's eldest son; ancestor of the great maritime nation of Sidon, later known as Phoenicia (present-day Syria and Lebanon).

Ancestor: Canaan. Genesis 10:15–19; 1 Chronicles 1:13

Heth ("terrible"). The second son of Canaan; ancestor of the Hittites. The chief area of their empire was in Asia Minor (Turkey).

Ancestor: Canaan. Genesis 10:15; 1 Chronicles 1:13

Jebus ("trodden under foot"). Listed as Canaan's third son. He was the Hamitic founder of the city Salem (Jerusalem). The Jebusites descended from him inhabited the Jerusalem vicinity prior to its conquest by King David.

Ancestor: Canaan. Genesis 10:6, 15; Joshua 15:63

Amrapel ("powerful people"). King of Shinar (Babylonia) who invaded and captured Sodom, and who held Abraham's nephew Lot and family as hostages. Later, he was defeated by Abraham's forces and rescued Lot.

Ancestor: Ethiopia. Genesis 14:1, 9

Melchizedek ("king of righteousness"). The godly priest-king of Salem (Jerusalem) to whom Abraham paid tithes. He was a type of Christ of the Old Testament.

Ancestor: Canaan. Genesis 14:18–20; Hebrews 5–7

Hagar ("wandering"). Abraham's African concubine and the mother of Ishmael. Because of the jealousy of Abraham's wife, Sarah, Hagar and her son, Ishmael, were cast out into the wilderness and nearly died, until an angel of the Lord saved them.

> Ancestor: Egypt. Genesis 16; 21:14–17

Ishmael ("God hears"). Son of Hagar; an expert archer. Married an Egyptian woman, had twelve sons who became the twelve tribes of the Ishmaelites (the first Arabians); from him the prophet Mohammed claimed African descent.

> Ancestor: Egypt. Genesis 16:11–16; Genesis 17:18–26

Keturah ("incense"). After the death of Sarah, Abraham took Keturah, an ethnic Ethiopian, as his wife. She was the mother of six sons, and all became prominent chieftains.

> Ancestor: Ethiopia. Genesis 25:1, 4

Midian ("strife"). One of the sons of Keturah; founder of one of the most powerful nations of the Midianites that occupied the Sinai and Arabian peninsulas.

> Ancestor: Ethiopia. Genesis 25:1–4; Genesis 36:35

Esau's Wives: Esau married three Hamitic women: Judith and Bashmath were Canaanites; Mahalath, Ishmael's daughter. Their descendants became known as Edomites, in the New Testament "Idumeans" (Greek).

> Ancestors: Egypt/Canaan. Genesis 26:34; Genesis 28:9

Amalek ("warlike"). Another grandson of Esau; half-brother of Kenaz, who was the ancestor of a large tribe of fierce desert tribesmen known as the Amalekites.

> Ancestor: Egypt/Canaan. Genesis 36:12, 16

Potiphar ("belong to the sun-god"). The captain of the guards in Pharaoh's court. He purchased Joseph as a slave from the Ishmaelite traders to whom his jealous brothers had sold him.

Ancestor: Egypt. Genesis 37:36, 39

Tamar ("palm"). A young Canaanite widow who disguised herself as a prostitute; lured Judah, her father-in-law, into an incestuous relationship; and became mother of twins, Perez and Zerah.
Ancestor: Canaan. Genesis 38:6–13; Ruth 4:12; Matthew 1:3
Perez ("bursting through"). Eldest son of Tamar by Judah, who became the "firstborn" offspring of Hamitic-Canaanite descent into the royal bloodline of Judah to David to Christ Jesus.

Ancestor: Canaan. Genesis 38:29; Luke 3:33

Asenath ("dedicated to god Neit"). Daughter of Potipherah, the chief priest at Heliopolis, and the Egyptian wife of Joseph.

Ancestor: Egypt. Genesis 41:45, 50; Genesis 46:20

Manasseh ("causing to forget") and **Ephraim** ("doubly fruitful"). The two sons of Asenath by Joseph. Their grandfather Jacob adopted them as his own sons. Manasseh and Ephraim were the African forefathers of the two most prominent tribes of the Israelites.

Ancestor: Egypt. Genesis 41:51; Genesis 48; Joshua 16:4–9; Joshua 17

Jethro ("his excellence"). A Midianite priest and Moses's father-in-law, who taught Moses to delegate responsibilities to his assistants.

Ancestor: Ethiopia. Exodus 3:1; Exodus 18:1–12

Zipporah ("little bird"). Moses's Ethiopian wife and the daughter of Jethro. Their sons were Gershom and Eliezer. When God sought to kill Moses because Eliezer had not been circumcised, Zipporah intervened.

The Egyptians introduced circumcision and embalming customs to the world.

Ancestor: Ethiopia. Exodus 2:21; Exodus 4:24–25

Joshua ("Jehovah is salvation"). Moses's successor who led the conquest of Canaan/Israel. A couple of well-known events of the Old Testament Book of Joshua were the fall of Jericho and the battle in Ajalon Valley, where the sun stood still. Joshua was a "great" grandson of Asenath, the African wife of Joseph.

Ancestor: Egypt. Exodus 17:9–14; Joshua; Deuteronomy 31:1–23

Caleb ("dog"). A Kenizzite prince and Moses's hand-picked leader to spy out the Promised Land. Caleb and Joshua were the only Egyptian-born survivors to enter Canaan; the others died in the desert.

Ancestor: Egypt/Canaan. Numbers 13:6; Joshua 14–15

Bezaleel ("in the shadow of Jehovah"). The chief architect whose skills were derived by the Spirit of God; he designed and constructed the Tabernacle and the Ark of the Covenant. He was a great grandson of Caleb.

Ancestors: Egypt/Canaan. Exodus 31:2–5; Exodus 36:1–2

Balaam ("a pilgrim"). A Midianite soothsayer hired by the king of Moab to curse the Israelites trespassing their land. Instead, messages by order of Jehovah and uttered by Balaam's talking donkey compelled him to bless them.

Ancestor: Ethiopia. Numbers 22–24; Numbers 31:8

Rahab ("broad"). A prostitute at Jericho (in Canaan) who hid the Israelite spies in her home and helped them capture the city. An ancestor of David and Jesus.

Ancestor: Canaan. Joshua 2; Joshua 6:17–25; Matthew 1:5

Adonibezek ("lord of lighting Bezek"). A king of Bezek captured by Joshua's forces who boasted he had mutilated and killed seventy kings. Likewise, he was mutilated and put to death.

Ancestor: Canaan. Judges 1:5–7

Othniel ("lion of God"). Caleb's nephew who, after the death of Joshua, liberated his people from foreign domination. Othniel, a Kenizzite, judged Israel for forty years.

Ancestors: Egypt/Canaan. Judges 1:13; Judges 3:8–11

Jarha ("free"). An African slave belonging to a man of Judah, Shehan. Because the master had no sons, he gave Jarha his freedom to marry his daughter in order to maintain the family bloodline in the tribe of Judah.

Ancestor: Egypt. 1 Chronicles 2:34–35

Salma ("firmness"). Son of Caleb, the Judahite and founder of the little town of Bethlehem in Judah (Israel), the birthplace of Jesus, David, and Jesse.

Ancestor: Canaan, Ham's fourth son. 1 Chronicles 2:51, 54

Cush-Rishathaim ("Ethiopian of double wickedness"). A powerful king of Mesopotamia (Babylonia) who dominated Israel for eight years until its deliverance by Othniel in 1367 BC.

Ancestor: Ethiopia, Ham's oldest son. Judges 3:7–10

Jael ("wild goat"). A Kenite, Heber's wife, who killed Sisera, the Canaanite general, when he took refuge in her tent after a humiliating defeat by the Israelites.

Ancestor: Ethiopia. Judges 4:17–22; Judges 5:6, 24

Gideon ("great warrior"). A farmer turned military hero who defeated an army of 135,000 Midianites with only 300 unarmed men. Later, he became judge over Israel from 1162–1122 BC. Gideon was a "great" grandson of Asenath and Joseph.

Ancestor: Ethiopia. Judges 6–8

Abimelech ("father of the king"). Son of Gideon and a Hivite woman. He slaughtered sixty-nine of his seventy brothers and then proclaimed himself the first king of Israel for three years (at Shechem).

Ancestors: Ethiopia/Canaan. Judges 8–9

Delilah ("dainty"). The beautiful Philistine woman from Sorek who was loved by Samson. After three drills, she discovered the secret of his strength was his uncut hair. When Samson fell asleep, she cut it off and turned him over to his enemies.

Ancestor: Egypt. Judges 16

Jesse ("Jehovah exists"). David's father; a great grandson of Rahab, the Afro-Canaanite heroine of the Old Testament; an ancestor of Jesus.

Ancestor: Canaan. Ruth 4:17–22; Matthew 1:5

Agag ("warlike"). Wicked king of the Amalekites who was captured; his life was spared by King Saul, but he was later hacked to death by Prophet Samuel.

Ancestor: Egypt/Canaan. 1 Samuel 15

David ("beloved"). Israel's second and greatest monarch; a shepherd, musician, poet, and military strategist. A man described by Jehovah himself as "A man after my own hearth" (Acts 13:22). He reigned from 1010–970 BC. His son Solomon and the nineteen kings of Judah descended from him were lineal "great" grandsons of Africans Tamar and Rahab, and they were ancestors of Jesus the Messiah.

Ancestor: Canaan. 1 Samuel 16; 2 Samuel; Matthew 1:1–17

Goliath ("an exile"). The Palestine giant-warrior who was over nine feet tall and defied the forces of Israel for forty days. He was finally confronted and slain by a teenage shepherd boy named David with a stone and a sling.

Ancestor: Egypt. 1 Samuel 17

Ahimelech ("brother of a king"). The high priest of Canaanite town of Nob who befriended David when he fled from King Saul's death squad.

Ancestor: Canaan. 1 Samuel 21–22

Doeg ("anxious"). The Edomite leader of Saul who executed Ahimelech and all eighty-four priests, as well as all the inhabitants and animals at Nob for aiding David on Saul's order.

Ancestors: Egypt/Canaan. 1 Samuel 22

Hiram ("my brother is the exalted"). King of Sidon (Phoenicia) from 980–947 BC. An ally of Kings David and Solomon who provided skilled craftsmen and materials to erect David's palace and Solomon's temple.

Ancestor: Canaan. 2 Samuel 5:11; 1 Kings 5; 1 Kings 9:10–14

Uriah ("Jehovah is my light"). A Hittite (Canaanite). The husband of Bathsheba and an elite commander in David's army. Because David had committed adultery with Uriah's wife, he ordered Uriah to be sent to the front line of battle to get him killed so that he could take Bathsheba as his wife.

Ancestor: Canaan. 2 Samuel 11

Absalom ("father of peace"). A son of David who led a rebellion against his father.

Ancestor: Canaan. 2 Samuel 13–19

Rephaim Giant ("powerful"). A Philistine giant warrior with twelve toes and twelve fingers; slain in battle by Jonathan, David's nephew.

Ancestor: Egypt. 2 Samuel 21:20–21

Solomon ("peace"). Son of David by Bathsheba; succeeded his father as third king of a united Israel for forty years (970–930 BC). World-famed for his wisdom and wealth. Hundreds of psalms and proverbs are ascribed to Solomon. He was an ancestor of Jesus.

Ancestor: Canaan. 1 Kings 1:11; 1 Kings 2:11; 2 Chronicles 1–9; Matthew 1:6–7

Makeda ("oath"), **Queen of Sheba.** The Sabean-Arabian monarch who visited King Solomon and was amazed by his wisdom and wealth. Jesus remarked about the queen's faith for traveling hundreds of miles by camels to learn more about the God whom Solomon worshipped.

Ancestor: Ethiopia. 1 Kings 10:1–10; Matthew 12: 42

Hadad ("thunderer"). A prince of Edom who, as a child, escaped the orders to exterminate all Edomite males carried out by Joab, David's general.

Ancestors: Egypt/Canaan. 1 Kings 11:14–22, 25

Tahpenes ("grandeur"). The Egyptian queen whose sister became the wife of Hadad, the Edomite prince.

Ancestor: Egypt. 1 Kings 11:18–20

Shishak. The first Libyan pharaoh of Egypt. He invaded Judah and subdued the capital Jerusalem during the reign of King Rehoboam.

Ancestor: Libya. 1 Kings 11:40; 2 Chronicles 12:1–9

Rehoboam ("freer of the people"). King Solomon's son; caused the kingdom to be divided into two nations, Israel (northern kingdom) and Judah (southern kingdom). He reigned as Judah's first king for some seventeen years (931–913 BC). He was an ancestor of Jesus.

> Ancestor: Canaan. 1 Kings 11:43; 1 Kings 12; Matthew 1:7

Asa ("physician"). The third king of Judah and the great grandson of Solomon. He was a Godly ruler for most of his forty-one-year reign. He was an ancestor of Jesus.

> Ancestor: Canaan. 1 Kings 15:8–16:29; Matthew 1:7–8

Zerah ("rising of light"). Ethiopian king and general during the days of King Asa; became the first military leader to amass a million-man army.

> Ancestor: Ethiopia.2 Chronicles 14

Nadab ("liberal"). Son and successor of Jeroboam as the second king of Israel; reigned less than two years (910–909 BC). Nadab was the first monarch of the northern kingdom of African descent. His mother was an Egyptian princess named Ano. (one of Jeroboam's secondary wives).

> Ancestor: Egypt. 1 Kings 15:25–31

Jezebel ("unexalted"). A Sidonian queen of Israel; introduced worship of Baal to Israel. Mother of Israel's kings Ahaziah and Jehoram, as well as Athaliah, queen of Judah.

> Ancestor: Canaan. 1 Kings 16:31; 1 Kings 18:4–21

Jehoshaphat ("Jehovah is judge"). Son of Asa, a "good" king who made many religious reforms during his reign as fourth king of Judah. An ancestor of Jesus.

> Ancestor Canaan. 1 Kings 22:41–50; Matthew 1:8

Naaman ("pleasantness"). A Syrian general who was healed of leprosy by bathing in the River Jordan seven times, as instructed by prophet Elisha.

> Ancestor: Canaan. 2 Kings 5; Luke 4:27

Athaliah ("Jehovah is strong"). The only woman to rule over Judah. After the death of her husband, King Jehoram, and later her son, King Ahaziah, Athaliah murdered her grandchildren and crowned herself queen of Judah, ruling for six years (841–835 BC).

> Ancestor, Canaan. 2 Kings 8:26; 2 Kings 11

Isaiah ("Salvation of Jehovah"). Considered the greatest Old Testament prophet. He predicted the coming of Christ the Messiah. His father, Amoz, was of Judahite/Canaanite lineage, and his uncle was the Israelite King Uzziah.

> Ancestor: Canaan.2 Kings 19:2, 20; Isaiah

So ("lifted up"). The Ethiopian pharaoh of Egypt whom King Hosea of Israel begged for military aid when the Israelites rebelled against Assyrian rule.

> Ancestor: Ethiopia. 2 Kings 17:4–7

Hezekiah ("Jehovah is strength"). The twelfth king of Judah (716–687 BC) and a religious reformer. He restored the Temple and was an ancestor of Jesus.

> Ancestor: Canaan.2 Kings 18–20; Matthew 1:9–10

Tirhakah ("exalted"). Egypt's last pharaoh of Ethiopian descent. He led a successful campaign against the Assyrians during the time of Hezekiah. Tirhakah, also known as Tahatqa.

> Ancestor: Ethiopia.2 Kings 19:9; Isaiah 37:9

Josiah ("Jehovah supports"). The sixteenth king of Judah. During his reign (640–609 BC), the Book of Deuteronomy was discovered. He was a God-fearing leader and an ancestor of Jesus Christ.

Ancestor: Canaan. 1 Kings 13:2; 2 Kings 22; Matthew 1:10–11

Zephaniah ("Jehovah has treasurer"). An Old Testament prophet who authored the Book of Zephaniah. He was son of Cushi ("Ethiopian") and was a great grandson of Hezekiah.

Ancestors: Ethiopia/Canaan. Zephaniah 1:1

Necho ("holy"). Egyptian pharaoh who defeated and slay Josiah, the king of Judah, in battle at Megiddo.

Ancestor: Egypt. 2 Chronicles 35:20–21

Zedekiah ("Jehovah my righteousness"). The twentieth and last king of Judah (597–586 NC) who was placed on the throne by Nebuchadnezzar. An ancestor of Jesus the Messiah.

Ancestor: Canaan. 2 Kings 24:18–25:7; 2 Chronicles 36:11–21

Evil-Merodach ("man of the god Marduk"). The king of Babylonia who released King Jehoiachin of Judah after thirty-seven years' imprisonment.

Ancestor: Ethiopia. 2 Kings 25:27–30; Jeremiah 52:31–34

Ebed-Melech ("servant of the king"). An Ethiopian guard in the service of King Zedekiah who rescued Prophet Jeremiah from a muddy dungeon, saving his life.

Ancestor: Ethiopia. Jeremiah 38:7–12; Jeremiah 39:16

Hophra ("crocodile"). Pharaoh of Egypt (589–570 BC) who aided King Zedekiah in his rebellion against Assyrian rule. Greek: APRIES

Ancestor: Egypt. Jeremiah 44:30

Belshazzar ("god Bel protect the king"). Babylonian king who was warned of his doom by divine handwriting on a wall, which was interpreted by Prophet Daniel.

Ancestor: Ethiopia. Daniel 5

Haman ("magnificent"). An Agagite (Edomite) and prime minister of Persia's King Xerxes. After Haman's foiled plot to exterminate all the Jews in the kingdom, he and his ten sons were hanged on the gallows he had erected for Jews.

Ancestors: Egypt/Canaan. Esther 3 - 9

Geshem ("rainstorm"). An Arab chieftain who attempted to sabotage Prophet Nehemiah's plan to rebuild the walls of Jerusalem.

Ancestor: Egypt. Nehemiah 2:9

Kings of Judah (Southern Kingdom)The nineteen Judean rulers were descendants of kings David and Solomon, and forebears of Jesus Christ: Rehoboam, Abijam, Asa, Jehoshaphat, Jehoram, Ahaziah, Joash, Amaziah, Uzziah, Jotham, Ahaz, Hezekiah, Manasseh, Amon, Josiah, Jehoahaz, Jehoiakim, Jehoiachin, Zedekiah.

Ancestor: Canaan. I Kings 11 - 2 Kings 24

New Testament

The Holy Family: Jesus; his mother, Mary; and her husband, Joseph (Jesus's foster father) were all direct descendants of African Hamites Tamar and Rahab. Joseph's royal Davidic lineage extended from King David's son, King Solomon, and through the succeeding nineteen kings of Judah, to Jesus. Mary's humble Davidic lineage derived from Nathan, another son of David, to Jesus (Matt. 1:1–17; Luke 3:23–38; 2 Sam. 5:14; 1 Chron. 3:5; Luke 3:31).

Ancestor: Canaan. Genesis 10:6, 15; New Testament

James the Just ("supplanter"). One of Jesus's brothers who became a believer after having witnessed the Lord's resurrection. He was installed as chief minister at the Church in Jerusalem, and he authored the epistle bearing his name.

Ancestor: Canaan. Matthew 13:55; James

Jesus's Siblings: Jesus's other brothers were Joseph, Simon and Jude, also he had several sisters. Jude wrote the New Testament epistle of Jude.

Ancestor: Canaan. Matthew 13:55; Mark 6:3; Jude

Herodian Dynasty. The Herods were a family of Idumeans (Edomites), who, under Roman control, ruled over Judea (Judah), Palestine, and Syria at the time of Jesus's birth until nearly seven decades after his earthly demise (37 BC–AD 100).

Herod the Great ("heroic"). The founder and first king who reigned 37–4 BC. It was this Herod who tried to kill the infant Jesus (Matthew 2:1–19; Luke 1:5).

Herod Archelaus. The eldest son of Herod the Great. He ruled at the time Mary, Joseph, and infant Jesus were exiles in Egypt (Matt. 2:19–23).

Herod Antipas. The youngest son of Herod the Great, who put John the Baptist to death (Matt. 14:1–12; Mark 6:14–29).

Herod Agrippa I. A grandson of Herod the Great who executed Apostle James and placed Apostle Peter on death row (Acts 12:1–24).

Herod Agrippa II. A great grandson of Herod the Great. He presided at the trial of Apostle Paul at Caesarea. He was the last ruler of the dynasty from AD 50–100 (Acts 25:13–26; Acts 26).

Herodias. Granddaughter of Herod the Great. She first married her uncle, Herod Philip, and then left him to marry his brother, Herod Antipas. John the Baptist denounced this union as illegal and incestuous (Matt. 14:3; Mark 6:17).

Bernice. Daughter of Agrippa I; consort/wife of her brother Agrippa II (Acts 25:13, 23).

Drusilla. Sister of Bernice and wife of Roman governor Felix (Acts 24:24–25).

Salome. The daughter of Queen Herodias who instructed by her mother to ask Herod Antipas (her stepfather) for the head of John the Baptist on a platter as a reward for her dancing (Matt. 14:1–12; Mark 6:14–29). Ancestors: Egypt/Canaan. Edomites descended from Jacob's son, Esau, and his African (and Canaanite) wives. Genesis 26:34; Genesis 28:9

Cyrenius ("of Cyrene"). The African governor of Syria and Judea (BC 4–AD 6) at the time Caesar Augustus ordered the census that brought Mary and Joseph to Bethlehem. ** Ancestor: Libya. Luke 2:2

Simon ("hearing") **of Cyrene** ("of Libya"). The Libyan-African who helped Jesus carry the cross on road to Mount Calvary. Halley's Bible Handbook (p. 452) quotes Matthew 27:32. "How proud, in heaven, throughout all eternity will be, to think he helped Jesus to bear his cross." Ancestor: Libya. Matthew 27:32; Mark 15:21

Ethiopian Treasurer. Upon returning from a trip to worship in Jerusalem, he was converted and baptized into the Christian faith by Philip the Evangelist. He introduced Christianity to Ethiopia and Africa (AD 31), prior to the first European convert, Lydia, at Philippi in Greece (AD 47). Ancestor: Ethiopia. Acts 8:26–40

Candace ("contrite"). The Ethiopian queen who permitted her chief officer to visit Jerusalem. Ancestor: Ethiopia. Acts 8:27

Simeon ("hearing") **the Niger** ("black") and **Lucius** ("of light"). African co-founders of the first (Gentile) Christian Church (Antioch, in Syria). Led by the Holy Spirit, they commissioned Paul and Barnabas for the first missionary journey. Ancestor: Libya. Acts 13:1–3

Aretas ("pleasing"). An Arabian king whose deputy sought to apprehend Paul, a novice convert of Christ at Damascus (Syria), but Paul's supporters let him down in a basket through an opening in the wall and escaped. Ancestor: Egypt. 2 Corinthians 11:32–33

Apollos ("a destroyer"). Egyptian disciple of John the Baptist, who was an eloquent speaker and preacher. Apollos was a partner of Paul, conveying God's message at Ephesus (Turkey) and Corinth (Greece). Ancestor: Egypt. Acts 18:24–28; Acts 19:1

Alexander ("man's helper") and **Rufus** ("red"). The two sons
of Simon the Libyan who were staunch Christian leaders
and missionaries in Jerusalem during the time of Paul.
Ancestor: Libya (Put). Mark 15:21; Romans 16:13

Linus ("net"). A Christian man at Rome from whom Apostle
Paul sent special greetings. According to the Book of Popes, Linus
was recorded as the second bishop (pope) of the Roman Catholic
Church and Empire (AD 67–76), succeeding Saint Peter.
Ancestor: Libya. Genesis 10:6; 2 Timothy 4:21

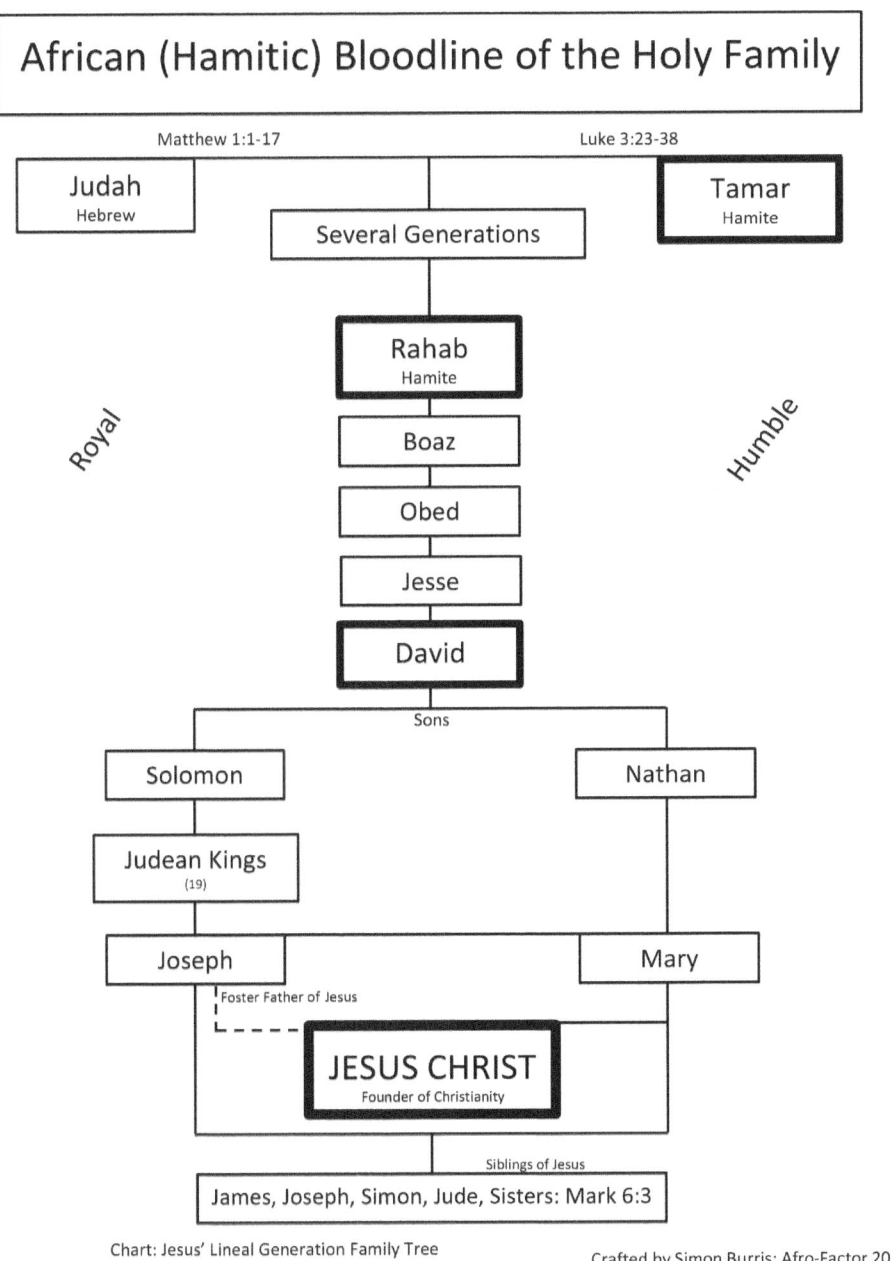

Chart: African (Hamitic) Bloodline of the Holy Family

Contemporary and Unnamed Egyptian Rulers (Pharaohs) of the Bible

Mentuhotep. Possibly the pharaoh to whom Abraham lied that his wife Sarah was only his sister. Genesis 12:10–20.

Ahmose I. The pharaoh who "knew not Joseph." He decreed to have Israelite babies put to death. He was probably the king who initiated Israelite enslavement. Exodus 1:8–22; Acts 7:18.

Hatshepsut. The pharaoh's daughter (Thutmose I) who rescued and raised infant Moses as her son. Years later, she ruled as the "first great queen in history." Exodus 2:5–10.

Thutmose III. The pharaoh who established Egypt as a superpower. He ruled during the time of Moses. He was the oppressor of the Israelites. Exodus 4:1–12:32.

The Exodus: 1446 BC

Akhenaten (Amenhotep IV). The first non-Israelite ruler to establish the One True God concept of religion (sun-god Aten). He ruled jointly with his wife, Nefertiti (1353–1336 BC) and was a contemporary of Israelite judge Othniel. Judges 3:8–11.

Tutankhamen. Akhenaton's son or son-in-law. He was the boy king who inherited the throne (1332 BC) at age nine, and he died at nineteen. King Tut's famed treasure-laden tomb was discovered in 1922. A contemporary of Judge Ehud. Judges 3:12–30.

Ramses the Great. The pharaoh regarded as one of the most successful and powerful kings of the Egyptian empire. He ruled some sixty-seven years during the time of judges Ehud and Shamgar. Judges 3:11–31

Cleopatra ("renowned"). The world's most famous queen and African monarch. She was the pharaoh celebrated for her beauty, charisma, military intellect, and amorous affairs with Roman Emperor Julius Caesar and, later, General Marc Antony. She reigned from 51 to 30 BC, a contemporary of King Herod the Great of Judea. Matthew 2; Luke 1:5.

Caesarion. The son of Cleopatra and Julius Caesar was the last native African pharaoh. He was three years old when proclaimed co-ruler with his mother (44–30 BC) A contemporary was Herod the Great.

Notes

1. Egyptians kings identified by names in the Bible are Shishak, So, Tirhakah, Necho, and Hophra.

2. The first legendary king of Egypt was Menes (3100 BC).

3. During the Napoleonic French Invasion of Egypt (1798–1799), many pharaoh images and monuments were defaced and destroyed by marauding soldiers.

Mentuhotep Osiride Statue

Ahmose I Statue Head

Hatshepsut

Thutmose III

Akhenaten

Tutankhamen

Ramses II

Necho (Knelling Statue)

Tirhakah (Taharqa)

Hophra (Apries)

Cleopatra VII

Caesarion, Cleopatra's son by Julius Caesar

List of Sources

Burris, Simon. *Black Nations/Black People.* Inglewood, CA: H. T. Tidings. A thematic booklet, 1992.

Evans, Williams. *The Great Doctrines of the Bible.* Chicago: Moody Press, 1912.

Funk, Issac. *Analytical Concordance of the Bible.* New York, 1917.

Halley, Henry H. *Halley's Bible Handbook.* Grand Rapids, MI: Zondervan Publishing House, 1959.

Leo Africanus. *History and Description of Africa, 1500s.* Hakluyt Society, 1896.

Bibles

Good News Translation (GNT). New York: American Bible Society, 1992.

King James Version (KJV). Nashville: Thomas Publishers, 1976.

New International Version (NIV). Colorado Springs, CO: International Society, 1989.

New Living Translation (NLT). Wheaton, IL: Tyndale House Publishers, Inc., 1996.

Suggested Readings
and Reviews

Barker, William. *Everyone in the Bible.* Old Tappan,
NJ: Fleming H. Revell Company, 1966.

Dunson, Alfred. *The Blackman in the Old Testament and
its World,* Trenton, NJ: Africa World Press, 1933.

Eerdman, William B. *Eerdman's Handbook of the Bible.* Grand
Rapids, MI: Zondervan Publishing Company, 1973.

Felder, Cane Hope. *The Original African Heritage
Study Bible, KJV.* Iowa Falls, Iowa, 1993.

www.ingramcontent.com/pod-product-compliance
Lightning Source LLC
Chambersburg PA
CBHW050356290526
45786CB00003B/1013